Escape

from

Management Land

A Journey Every Team
Wants Their Leader to Take

KEN CARNES AND DAVID COTTRELL

Escape
from
Management Land

A Journey Every Team Wants Their Leader to Take

Inquiries regarding permission for use of the material contained in this book should be addressed to:

CornerStone Leadership Institute
P.O. Box 764087
Dallas, TX 75376
888.789.LEAD

Printed in the United States of America
ISBN: 0-9788137-0-7

Credits

Design, art direction, and production	Melissa Monogue, Back Porch Creative, Plano, TX
	info@BackPorchCreative.com
Illustrations	Spencer Smith

This book is dedicated to those who have led in the past, are leading now, and those who aspire to be leaders in the future.

Successful leadership is a dynamic challenge. It is the result of many trials and painful errors, of strong mentoring and life-changing experiences. Even the greatest leaders occasionally have to escape from Management Land before returning to Leader Land.

May this book remind you how to make the most of every step of your leadership journey.

TABLE OF CONTENTS

THE ANNOUNCEMENT

It was one of the best days of Erik Walter's professional career.

"Congratulations! I am proud to tell you, you got the job!"

He could not believe the Vice President's words.

"You have prepared for this promotion for a long time," the VP continued at the other end of the line, "and the entire senior executive team is confident that you will do an outstanding job in your new position. We are looking forward to your leadership. You were the obvious choice because of how you've prepared yourself for the past five years for this moment."

Manager! It had been Erik's goal from the moment he was hired to work with the company. Now, the promotion he had worked so hard for finally happened. The reality still hadn't hit him, even as his friends and co-workers celebrated his announcement that afternoon.

"Man, you've worked hard for this one," said Ted Lane, one of his peers. "I know how many late nights you've put in and how you went above and beyond, time after time. You earned this job. Let me know if you need anything during your transition time."

"Way to go, Erik!" Toni Maynard shook his hand and gave him a congratulatory hug. "Couldn't have happened to a better guy! Proud of you!" she said.

As Erik prepared to leave the office, he noticed a hastily scrawled note on dark gray paper someone apparently had slipped onto his desk, probably while he was down the hall celebrating. He picked it up and was ready to toss it in the trash when he stopped to read its message:

"Are you just like all the others?"

The new manager frowned as he flipped the piece of paper, looking for some identifying markings. Nothing. "Wonder where this came from, and what it's about?" he said, finally deciding to slip it into his briefcase.

Returning home after celebrating his new position with the family, Erik's wife realized her husband was still on a high from the good news. Kristen whispered, "Go in and put your feet up while I put the kids to bed. I am so proud of you!"

"I'm still having a hard time believing it," Erik smiled, settling into his favorite chair. "And, aside from the new title, we have a chance to make more money. Don't know how much yet, but this is our first step up the proverbial corporate ladder!"

Propping his feet on the ottoman, Erik closed his eyes and tried to make sense of the thousands of ideas running through his head,

"Man, do I have plans," he thought to himself. "I actually have a team to lead … and I know I'll make a great manager. I have a million ideas, and our team will be recognized at next spring's annual corporate meeting.

Then his mind wandered to the strange note, but only for a moment. "No big deal," he thought, "probably just a prank. But who would write that and what are they really trying to say?"

Erik wasn't going to allow an anonymous note ruin his big day. "I don't know who 'the others' are, but I'm willing to guarantee our productivity will be through the roof! We'll knock our competition's socks off!"

After making his way to bed, his brain continued to race with new ideas and excitement. Lying in the quiet of early morning, Erik had visions of unprecedented success. "Within a few years, who knows? I could have an office on the 15th floor, a new house … Awesome."

An ambitious and hard-working rising star elevated to the next level of responsibility is nothing unusual. It is an earned rite of passage up the corporate ladder.

But, what about those affected by the promotion?

In the midst of all the celebrating earlier that afternoon, Erik was so exuberant after the announcement of his promotion, he never even noticed the expressions on the faces of five members of his soon-to-be-team.

Their excitement certainly didn't mirror Erik's. In fact, as quietly as possible, all had cleared their desks and left the office, not bothering to join in the celebration. They had good reason to avoid the celebration.

Their team had plenty of experience with new managers. Their past experiences gave them little cause to celebrate. If anything, this was another unknown quantity standing between them and their future career options. Instead of Erik's "here we go so hold on tight" excitement, they walked away thinking "here we go ... again."

"It's unsettling. No, downright scary," said Jason Brown, one of the stars of the team, as the five disillusioned workers walked toward their cars. "Who knows what he'll do? Oh, he's a nice enough guy, but we've had 'nice' before."

"You said it." Angela Martin rolled her eyes. "My feeling exactly. Nice doesn't cut it. I want him to tell me what's in it for me if I work my butt off. I'm not as young ... and as dumb ... as I used to be. We've all been doing pretty well ... even though we all get things done differently."

"I just want specifics," agreed Al Smith. "I'm willing to do almost anything ... as long as I know what we are trying to accomplish and why. I mean, we've seen everything, haven't we? The good, the bad and ...."

"The ugly." Morgan Thornton, the most outspoken of the group, finished his sentence ... "and, personally, thanks to combat experiences with some of our former bosses, I'm not as flexible as I used to be, either. I'm not as willing to give up big chunks of my life to work all hours on this job as I once was."

"Only time will tell," chimed in Harry Hemski, always the philosopher of the group. "In the meantime, I'm gonna enjoy the evening, come in tomorrow, and hope ... no pray ... for the best."

So, while Erik Walters and his family were celebrating his promotion, the members of his new team were bracing themselves for their first day with Erik as their new leader. They were preparing for the worst and hoping for the best.

Erik's optimism and his team's skepticism are not unusual. In fact, most new managers go into the job with the same enthusiasm as Erik but – for a variety of reasons – fail to achieve their dreams and goals. These failures are rarely because new managers do not have the competency and desire to become great leaders. However, they are often promoted without really knowing what they are getting into and what pitfalls to avoid.

The brief fable that follows is about Erik's journey, from those first exciting moments following the announcement of his promotion to the realities that come with successfully leading a group of diverse people to their highest potential.

Written to entertain and to teach, *Escape from Management Land* is a fictional and, at times, outlandish tale. But at some point in your career, you will find yourself in Management Land, struggling to escape.

This book is also written to show how even great leaders occasionally fall into the trap of Management Land and have to make the journey back to Leader Land.

Most readers will be able to relate to, and recall, personal experiences similar to those Erik encounters. However, rather than just depicting the situations and providing the symptoms to look for, this book offers the solutions you'll need to recognize and escape from actions that push even the best leaders back to Management Land from time to time.

Accompany Erik as he learns the invaluable, and often unforgettable, lessons about leadership he's about to learn. Then, decide if you're willing to do what it takes to escape Management Land and move into Leader Land.

After you've read this book, keep it handy. The lessons learned along Erik's journey are not easily digested in just one reading. Step away from the book. Then come back and, as you review them from time to time, they become even more valuable and, often, more applicable to your own situation.

Read, enjoy, learn, and have a great trip!

"On every journey you take, you are met with options.
At every fork in the road, you make a choice.
These are the decisions that shape your life."
– Mike DeWine, U.S. Senator, Ohio

It had taken Erik hours to work off the adrenaline of the day and finally close his eyes in the wee small hours. For what seemed only a few minutes, he had fallen into a deep sleep, but suddenly there was someone shouting his name.

"Erik. Erik Walters! Come on, man. Time's awasting," called the voice that sounded familiar although Erik couldn't pinpoint where it was coming from.

Startled and alarmed, Erik sat up. "All right," he said sleepily. "Give me a minute."

"There's no time, man. It's time to go. Right now," said a chorus of voices, still sounding familiar. But as Erik rubbed his eyes and looked around, he still couldn't see where they were coming from.

As his eyes focused and the faces came into view, one by one, Erik recognized the chorus of voices as several members of his new team, "What's up? I mean, what are you doing here? Time to go where?"

"We're off to see the Wizard," joked Harry. "Well, not really the Wizard. Thought I'd throw that in for dramatic effect. Just follow me."

"But where to?"

"To Management Land, of course," chorused the quintet – Jason, Angela, Al, Morgan and Harry. "When you were promoted today, you punched your ticket to Management Land and we're going to be your tour guides."

"I must be dreaming," said Erik, pinching himself. "Of course I am. I've been thinking of these people ever since I answered the call from the VP today, so, it's natural to see them in my dreams."

"You'll need shoes," Harry suggested, pointing to Erik's bare feet. "It could be rough going if you intend to travel like you are. But hurry. We have to be going."

After slipping on his running shoes and following behind the parade, Erik was deep in thought, trying to determine if what he was seeing and hearing was real or imagined. "Come to think about it, these guys didn't hang around too long after the announcement of my promotion," he thought. "In fact, they didn't seem too thrilled about the whole scene. So, isn't it logical that when I saw their less-than-excited expressions, I would subconsciously transfer them to my dreams? Yes, of course! That's it. A dream!"

"Hurry up," Angela hollered. "We don't have all night."

"I'm coming," Erik shouted back, picking up his pace.

Just then, they passed a sign: "Welcome to Management Land …
Home of Mediocrity," it read.

"So, what and where is Management Land?" the new manager
wanted to know.

"Well, here it is in a nutshell," said Morgan, stopping and turning
to confront Erik. "We've been through this new manager scene
more than once. We're not excited about going through it again.
In fact, we're all a little weary of new managers if you want to
know the truth. We've seen 'em come and we've seen 'em go.
We've seen a half dozen just like you in the past few years.

"All of them were excited and were anxious to set the world on
fire … just like you are right now. But I can tell you, breaking in
a new manager is no fun. In fact, most of us would rather have a
root canal than go though the pain of watching someone trying
to play new manager."

"You can say that again," said Jason, a 20-something working on
his MBA, joined in. "I've been around for the last two versions of
team manager and I'd rather be almost anywhere than sitting at
my desk, welcoming a new one."

"So, you all are not excited to see me," Erik surmised, wryly. "But,
I have worked hard for this promotion. I know I will be a great
manager for you."

"Ha. We've heard that before. Do you think anyone believes they
don't deserve a promotion? Every manager before you said the same
thing. And us not being excited to see you? That's an understatement.
Not only are we *not* excited, we're fed up, going through this same

cycle over and over again," Morgan continued. "So we're trying something new.

"Before you get too comfortable in your new corner office with your big leather chair and your granite-topped credenza with the ivy plant, we want to show you some of the choices our former managers have made – and what they did – mainly to us."

"Yeah," said Harry, "and after you've seen all that we want to show you, maybe you can understand why we weren't celebrating earlier today, and why you have to prove yourself to us."

"Prove myself?" Erik blurted, sounding slightly more arrogant than he intended, "but, I've got an MBA and several years ex ...."

"Yeah, yeah, yeah, but before we accept you as part of our team, you have to prove you care about us and can move our team forward," Harry interrupted. "Otherwise, we've all been there, done that and got the T-shirt. Too many times, new managers are all talk, platitudes, and so bent on using us to move to the next level, they lose sight of making our team better."

"That's why we've brought you here," Jason explained. You'll see. And once you've seen it, you'll never forget Management Land ... or the land beyond, either."

"Land beyond? You mean we're leaving the planet?"

"Nothing quite so intergalactic," Jason promised. "Just a place every team wants their leader to reach." He stopped, noticing Erik's puzzled expression. Then he continued. "Just hang with us," he instructed. "We'll take good care of you."

Erik surveyed Management Land's picturesque horizon. To him, this place looked like any other sprawling landscape. It was resort-like – with streams, mountains and valleys surrounded by sandy beaches lapped with crystalline blue surf. "Not bad. In fact, it looks like a wonderful place to vacation," he said, almost under his breath but loudly enough for the group to hear.

"Ah, but looks can be deceiving, as you may already know," Morgan reminded as she led the group around the bend to a natural staircase that descended into a canyon-like expanse.

"Yes, it may look wonderful to you," Angela said through clamped teeth, "but we know from experience, this beautiful place is also where managers who have no business managing are sent."

Erik's stunned expression urged more information. "But, maybe I'm not like your other managers. Maybe I can do a better job at managing."

"We've all been through this drill before … more than once," Angela continued, her facial expression mirroring her negative feelings. "We've had managers who thought they were going to be the greatest, just like you're saying. But, we do not need a manager who is happy to be in Management Land. We need a leader who wants to help us accomplish our goals. "

Then Al took over. "We're all working our rears off, making our numbers and we've just adjusted to one management style – whether good or bad – and then we find ourselves breaking in a new manager. Like Forrest Gump said, 'Life's a box of chocolates … you never know what you're going to get.' In our case, new managers are just like chocolates."

"Except you can't poke them in the middle to find out what flavor you're going to get," Jason chimed in. "But more often than not, lately, all we've gotten has been a bunch of nuts ... or worse."

"Because of our past experience," Morgan said, rolling her eyes, "bringing in a new manager is like taking our careers and throwing them into a black hole. Unfortunately, if the new manager is weak, our careers will never be the same, or they may be ruined forever. You see, we are a reflection of our leader, and we don't like the reflection we have seen with the last wave of managers."

"Which is why we brought you here," Angela interrupted. "We want to show you some of the mistakes our past managers have made, and, even though it may not sound like it, we really want you to be successful and a great leader. That would make all our jobs much better!"

"Because we don't want to go through the same awful experiences again," Al said resolutely. "Once you see what we have to show you, then you can either be good or great. Although we're not expecting miracles at this point."

"Or you can be like one of the managers we've had before," Morgan continued, "managers who sabotaged our spirit, took our efforts for granted – as well as our careers – kept us from making deadlines and quotas. You name it, we've seen it. Some of those managers – and this is putting it nicely – did us no favors and nothing for our futures."

"Or our attitudes about work," said Angela, kicking a small stone off the path as she spoke.

"Sounds like you guys have had some ... some challenging experiences," Erik said, sympathetically.

"Challenging may be your assessment," Al retorted, "but we have other words for what we've been through ... words you're probably not ready to hear right now. Just remember, your leadership will have more impact on our success than anything else. You set the pace around here and it can be positive or negative."

"But, I'm open," Erik protested. "One thing I'm known for is being a straight shooter."

Now Harry rolled his eyes. "Don't think being a straight shooter is the key," he said, "because we've heard that song and dance before, too – an open-door policy, team player, proactive and on and on, ad nauseam. But because of our recent experiences with new managers, we see those proclamations as just so many words, unless proven otherwise. And I can tell you, we're batting a thousand in that category.

"But, now it's time we started the 50-cent tour of this place. And we want to remind you of a few things before our first stop," Harry said, taking the lead. "First of all, we're going to show you some of our previous managers. They were all excited about their promotions, just like you, but 'things' happened and they lost sight of what was important."

"Yep, they're all here, all right," Jason nodded.

"Secondly, we want you to notice that there are no teams in Management Land," Harry continued.

"No teams?" Erik protested.

"That's right. No teams. And there's also no spirit, no record-breaking performances, no awards, no forward progress. Quite frankly, the work styles here fall well below what most of us want for ourselves. You'll see what we mean."

Now it was Morgan's turn. "We also want to show you the impact a poor manager has on the spirit and the choices available to employees." Her voice was sharp, almost razor-like, as she spoke. "You're going to see a lot of people just putting in their time. Where they were once really jazzed about what they were doing in their jobs, they're now just marking time ... sort of like zombies."

Erik interrupted. "Come on. This can't be all the manager's fault. I mean, what about individual initiative? What about their responsibilities to be the best? They may be making some bad choices."

"You're right! They do have responsibilities and choices," Morgan continued. "That's the reason why our turnover is so high. A lot of people choose to leave. We are here to tell you directly. Now listen closely. You're the manager and you have a tremendous amount of influence on your team's choices, job satisfaction and productivity. Probably much more than you realize."

"Most people who leave our organization did not leave because of pay or benefits. They didn't leave because of schedules or workload." Morgan was definitely on a roll. "They left because the person who was supposed to be their leader was not meeting their needs. They'd had enough of the Management Land scene!

Her voice was passionate as she spoke. "It's heartbreaking when we see it because we were almost there ourselves, several times. We're hoping this tour of Management Land has the same impact for you."

"Okay, okay. I'm beginning to get the picture," the new manager said, "but you're judging me before I've even had a chance to show you how I lead. I promise I'll be better than what you've had before. I'll be a good manager, or die trying."

"We hear what you're saying and we want to believe you," Angela said, "but that's not good enough. We don't need a good manager. We need a great leader."

"So, what's the difference?" Erik interrupted again.

"You'll see at the end of our trip. However, just to be fair, toward the end of our tour, we're going to ask you some questions. So be ready," Angela warned as they moved ahead.

"Agreed. I'll answer the questions and we'll talk about my answers. I'd like to have your input, as well," Erik said, struggling for compromise.

"We'll talk only if we like the answers you offer," Morgan said, explaining the group's conditions. "Remember, we've been around this block several times before, and what we're looking for is a leader, not just a manager," Morgan said. "We also have the option of leaving you in Management Land, hoping the organization will rethink their choice about who's got the right stuff to take charge of our group," she teased.

"So, you're holding me hostage?"

"Well, not exactly," Morgan continued. "We just want to make sure we're all on the same page before you start leading our team."

"Man, I've had some doozies in the dream department, but this takes the cake," Erik mumbled under his breath.

"You can think so all you want, but for now you need to follow us. You'll find out whether this is a dream or a full-fledged nightmare," Jason smiled and beckoned for his new boss to follow his lead.

"If dreams die, life is a broken-winged bird that cannot fly.
If dreams go, life is a barren field, frozen with snow."
            · – Langston Hughes, author

O ne thing you'll need to know before we go much farther," said Jason, turning to push a stray branch out of his way. "Management Land is reactive."

"Like a volcano?" Erik asked.

"The group laughed. "Well …."

"Yeah, totally," Angela agreed. "What we mean is there's nothing proactive about any part of this place. There's no planning, strategy or contingency."

"No Plan B," Jason added.

"Every day's a fire drill," nodded Harry, "and surprises occur hourly. Most importantly, Management Land is reactive to the manager. In every stop, you will notice that the leader creates the environment. Everyone follows the leader, which in Management Land is not a good deal."

About that time, the group moved beyond the lush landscape of Management Land. They were suddenly confronted by the gapping mouth of a cavernous outcropping.

Inside was dark and depressing, and as the group had promised, there was a corner office surrounded by cubicles populated by desks and workers, all pale and slow-moving. The cave's darkness had siphoned any color from the scene, which unfolded in shades of gray, punctuated by dim, naked light bulbs hanging randomly from the low ceiling.

"Welcome to Apathy Cave," Harry whispered as he showed Erik inside the gaping cavern. "The corner office belongs to Bruce, our manager three or four years ago. He'll never move from that office. And the staff you see today – or at least most of it – has been here for a long time, except for some of the new transfers from other places around here."

"Why do you say 'most of it?'" asked Erik.

"Because about half of the staff isn't here," explained Harry. "If you spend much time in Apathy Cave, you get used to a lot of absenteeism and tardiness. In fact, almost everybody in here quit their jobs years ago. But, unfortunately they didn't tell anyone. They just kept on coming to work."

"Or, not. Because most of these people work a WIFLI schedule," Jason joined in.

"WIFLI? That's a new one," Erik pondered.

"Means 'Whenever I Feel Like It,'" explained Morgan. "That's the mantra here in the cave."

"Furthermore, the enthusiasm has been zapped out of the cave," Harry continued. "Listen. All you hear is sighing. There's little conversation … laughter, camaraderie or team spirit. They don't even have enough enthusiasm to throw a birthday party around here," he said, pointing to an uneaten birthday cake on the table in their well-used break room.

"But, nobody's really doing anything, other than waiting for the clock to tell them it is time to go home," Erik observed. "Or at least they don't look like they're doing anything. No wonder they call this Apathy Cave."

As he looked around the cavern, he saw desk after desk stacked with paper. "Looks like a paperwork swamp," he quipped but quickly stopped smiling when he saw the expressions on his guides' faces.

"We'll get to that issue later," Morgan chided. "Meanwhile, focus on this scene. Some of these people are exactly that. Bogged down. Others are just plain broken. I'll also point out there's little creativity here. And most of the team sees this as their last stop. They've just lost hope."

Erik continued to scan the cave. There were no books, no training rooms and no learning going on, except for one guy, over in the corner, catching up on his fantasy football team results on his computer.

There was also a conspicuous absence of awards on the wall or posters encouraging excellence.

"What's that unsightly mess over there?" interrupted Erik.

"It looks like a mass of discarded company awards, promotion letters, mixed in with easels, flipcharts and storyboards with great ideas sketched on them that never were used. The endless pile of debris started in a dark corner of the cave, were dead-end careers had been discarded. The sense of lost dreams and unrealized potential created such an indescribable feeling of hopelessness that filled much of the cave," Angela commented. "It's like everybody is on hold. No forward movement, nobody's growing and nobody's reaching any higher than their inbox when paychecks are distributed."

"There's one more thing I need to tell you," Harry offered. "You can't see it, but there's been some bad hiring around here."

"Bad hiring?" Erik looked puzzled yet again.

"A penchant for hiring people who look exactly like everybody else," Harry continued, "and I don't mean physically."

The others chuckled at this statement as they noted Harry's girth and Morgan's tall, slender frame.

"No, I mean people who have the same backgrounds and skill sets. There is not enough diversity to push the team forward so everyone continues to mark time instead of moving ahead," said Harry.

Erik shook his head again. "I can understand why the good people on the team would try to get out of here as soon as they could."

Al, usually the quietest of the quintet, spoke up. "Yeah, there is no one leading the team to step up the pace," he said. "In Apathy Cave, there's very little momentum or movement, and nobody really cares. In my humble opinion, this place is the worst you'll see on our trip."

"The cave people only care about punching the clock, going home and leaving it all behind them," Morgan said, finishing Al's thought. "This particular environment encourages cynicism and maintaining the status quo. You can't rock the boat while you are in the cave!"

"Meanwhile, the boat drifts aimlessly," Harry continued, "and any enthusiasm among the troops soon becomes total indifference. As you can see, everybody just sort of zombies out."

Erik walked on in silence. He'd never had this type of experience before.

None of the people in the cavern seemed to be interested enough to notice the visitors as they surveyed the scene. "Geez," Erik said after spending a few minutes inside the musty office, "this is one place where watching paint dry would be exciting. I've never seen anything like it."

Then, Erik's expression changed. "Wait a minute! You said careers hit a dead end here, but I see young people as well as those who look like they're old enough to draw Social Security. What's the story?"

"Uninvolved managers who do not have a clear vision of what they want the team to accomplish can kill careers for anyone … not just the more experienced workers," Morgan responded. "And without strong, caring and concerned leadership, it doesn't take long to turn energetic fast-trackers into the unengaged zombies you see here."

"I've never seen anything like this before," Erik whispered again.

"Well, we have and that's one reason you're here," Harry said. "Look over there. If you watch for just a few minutes, while the people at the desks appear to be busy, they don't know what to do. Nobody ever gives them feedback, so they do the no-brainer tasks until someone gives them something else to do, except no one does.

"That guy – Paul is his name – was an up-and-comer. Now look at him."

Over in one corner of the cavern, a pale and drawn Paul sat transfixed in front of a computer screen, playing computer games. But Erik noticed something very strange. Every time Paul came close to winning, he would start a new game.

"Why does he do that?" Erik asked. "Why doesn't he just finish the game?"

In the background, a phone's weak ringing pierced the quiet, but nobody bothered to answer, it continued to ring and ring, until the caller apparently gave up.

"Because the overarching attitude of Apathy Cave is so saturated in cynicism, Paul is actually trying to lose," Angela explained knowingly.

"This is too surreal," Erik decided aloud. "What happened to Paul's enthusiasm and ambition?"

"Can't you see?" Angela asked. "He's not even aware that he is in the cave. He has spent so much time without any support or leadership, he is immune to his apathetic situation. He doesn't know how to escape. This time next week you'll find him in the exact same position, playing – and never winning – computer games at his desk."

Erik shook his head in disbelief. "But, if he were such an up-and-comer ...?"

"Doesn't matter," Morgan countered. "You could be the hardest-charging go-getter on the planet, but if you're surrounded by people who don't care, you grow tired of butting into barriers. Eventually, even those with the best intentions begin buying into the status quo."

"Regardless how many good ideas you have, how much time you spend doing your job or how eager you are to move ahead, it just isn't going to happen in Apathy Cave," Harry explained, shaking his head and remembering his own equally painful experiences.

"So, this is what a dead zone looks like," Erik empathized.

"Not dead, but close to it. Look, there's a very talented person," Angela said, pointing to a woman wearing dark glasses and sitting at a desk against the opposite wall of the cave. "That's Jane and this was her first job. She's here in the cave because nobody provided her with any direction and she doesn't know any better. With just a little guidance, she could have gone gangbusters for the organization. She was smart, outgoing and had all the right stuff to be successful, but here in the cave, she lost her vision, her ability to see the big picture as well as the opportunities in her future."

"But, in fairness to Jane," said Harry, coming to the pale woman's defense, "she never had a chance. This is all she knows."

Erik shook his head again. "This place is beginning to really creep me out, but what I can't figure out is why these people keep coming to work, especially if it's a dead end."

"The manager sets the pace," Harry said, "although you already know that. See that guy on the treadmill? His name's Ted."

"Sure … he's about the only thing moving in this place, but at least he's moving," Erik said, rubbing his chin. "Why is he on the treadmill?"

"Well, there was a treadmill in the break room when Ted came to the cave and he got into the habit of spending most of his day on it. He is worn out by the time he goes home yet he has not made any progress all day," Angela explained.

"Ted's logged more than 1,000 miles on that dang treadmill, so he may be ready to run the New York Marathon," Morgan offered, "but, in reality, just like a pet hamster, Ted's going nowhere."

"Yep. Ted keeps going and going and going … like the battery bunny," Harry said sullenly. "Trouble is, no matter how fast or slow he goes, he's going to be on that treadmill for years, unless …."

"Unless a strong leader comes in and starts channeling Ted's energy in a more productive direction," Jason said, "and from our own experiences, we all know that's probably not going to happen in the cave anytime soon."

"But surely, Ted is bright enough to figure things out," Erik said, struggling to make sense of this whole scene.

"You're right. Ted is bright and, like all team members, he has the responsibility of taking care of his own career path, but since he's been working here, he's allowed himself to narrow those choices to the point that he's torn between staying on the treadmill or taking a big risk and asking for a transfer out of the cave," Jason continued.

"If it weren't so depressing in here, it'd be almost comical," Erik said in a barely audible tone.

"Remember what we told you up front. The people at every stop we will make are a reflection of their leader. Think about the people here," Al offered. "Most of them were willing to do what it took to be successful, but now it's like they are on the last voyage of the Titanic. Except, rather than sinking, this ship remains unmercifully afloat, without direction going nowhere."

"But, we *do* have places to go and people to see," chirped Angela, a welcome relief from the heavy feelings that were wafting through the dark, dank cavern. "So, if you've had a good look here, let's be on our way."

Erik looked relieved. "I believe I've had all of this place I can enjoy," he said wryly. "It has all the charm of City Morgue, and I can promise, I would never manage any of you into this Apathy Cave."

"Fortunately, most of the managers who come to the cave do not stay there," Harry explained. "They recognize that the place is dead and many of them spot the apathy right off. We have seen them escape by focusing on the important things and attacking the problems that exist in Apathy Cave. Once they do that and begin providing hope for the members of the team, they leave the cave and make their way over to Leader Land."

"I believe Erik's got the picture," Angela called back to her fellow team members, "but hard experience tells us, we can never be too sure."

"Exactly," Morgan leered. "Next stop."

APATHY CAVE

SYMPTOMS

- Non-caring, negative attitudes and environment.
- Problems are ignored and covered up. Excellence is an afterthought.
- Employees are afraid to make decisions because they are constantly second-guessed.
- Employees seem cynical and are disengaged from the organization's mission and values.
- Culture dominated by blame and justification, not solutions.
- Barriers to change and improvement are everywhere.
- Absenteeism, tardiness and lack of ownership and involvement are the rule.

EXIT STRATEGIES

- Identify your current legacy. *Are you in Apathy Cave? If today was your last day at work, what would your team say about you? What legacy will you leave?*
- Create a new personal and professional vision. Then constantly communicate that vision, connecting people to it.
- Identify the strengths of your team members and develop coaching plans, offering mentoring and support.
- Find and align with the positive. It's easier to be pulled down than it is to be pulled up.
- Create a climate of ownership, empower your team to act and then reward positive performance.

"The price of excellence is discipline.
The cost of mediocrity is disappointment."
– William Arthur Ward, College Administrator

Pausing to take a break before traveling to their next stop in Management Land, the group is curious about Erik's reaction.

"Man, I don't ever want to be anyplace like that again," he said between cooling sips of water from a bottle Morgan magically produced from her backpack, along with some fresh fruit. "But you don't have to worry. I'm not that kind of manager."

"Sorry, Erik, but we've heard the same promises before," Angela shot back. "We're all really old pros when it comes to managers with good intentions who never quite make the grade.

"Imagine how we felt when Bruce moved into our group and we began sizing up his management style," she continued. "If we all hadn't been working on a really awesome project left over from our last manager, we would have ended up in that cave with him. Luckily, we were all so focused on making a positive difference that we sort of, well, we – in a manner of speaking – ignored Bruce for the first several weeks he was there."

"It didn't take us too long to figure out what was going on," Al interjected. "I mean he would call meetings and show up late and occasionally never show at all. He didn't spend much time assessing our group or determining where our individual strengths could be plugged into his master plan ...."

"Mainly, because he didn't have one," Morgan laughed and then apologized. "Except it wasn't funny then, and it's even less funny now. Sorry."

Now it was Erik's time to speak. "I've seen managers like Bruce before, and you're all exactly right. Working for them can be excruciatingly painful. You're fired up and ready to go and then 'Poof!' Nothing happens. And nothing keeps happening until either you get tired of having the same nothing type of experience or the manager moves up or out."

"Exactly. Enter Apathy Cave," Harry added. "Been there, done that, and we're not willing to go there again."

"Okay, break time's over. We need to get moving," Angela announced. "We've still got a lot of ground to cover."

"But haven't we seen enough?" Erik objected. "Can't we go back where we came from?"

"As they say in show business, 'You ain't seen nothing yet,'" Al responded. "We're just getting started, so settle back, relax and enjoy the trip," he smirked.

After walking about 15 minutes, the group rounded a bend in the road to discover an idyllic setting, a far cry from their last stop. Just ahead, they could see someone fishing along an emerald blue lake. Another was napping peacefully, waiting for fish to take his hook.

"Why, this is beautiful," Erik exclaimed, not bothering to hide his relief. "This is like paradise, particularly when you compare it to Apathy Cave."

"Not so fast," Harry cautioned. "We have just entered the Valley of Comfort."

Erik looked puzzled. "I don't understand. Everybody looks so content, so comfortable, so ... so happy. I really like this place."

"Yeah," Jason snickered. "So do these people ... like it here, I mean, and, you're right. It's really comfortable here. See, there's Jim, an avid fisherman. He's been fishing this lake in the exact same spot for at least two years, since his new manager brought him here. The problem is that Jim's never caught a thing."

"So why does he keep fishing?" Erik wanted to know.

"Because he's comfortable doing things just like he always has," Angela answered. "The sad thing is, if he'd change just one thing – if he'd move just about 100 feet up the bank – he could catch more fish than he'd know what to do with."

"Sounds easy enough. Why doesn't he move?"

"Because he's comfortable where he is. He enjoys fishing where there are no fish. He keeps fishing there because he knows that a big one will not get away."

A light bulb went off in Erik's head. "Oh, I get it. He's frozen in his comfort zone and doesn't want to take the risk of moving up the bank where the fish might be because he is afraid to fish and fail?"

"You're getting pretty good at this," Harry chuckled, clapping him on the back, "but don't get a big head. You're not even close to passing 'Go!'

"You probably know from personal experience," said Harry, "that it's easier to stay in your comfort zone than it is to take risks and do something different. It's human nature. Unfortunately, staying in your comfort zone results in mediocrity in every part of your performance. For most of us, taking risks is hard and sometimes painful, unless, of course, your leader – your manager – sets the example and builds in some baby steps along the way when change occurs."

"Or prepares you for the journey," Morgan interjected.

"I agree with that," Erik nodded. "If there are risks, it's up to the manager to create an environment where taking risks doesn't mean putting your job on the line if things don't work out. And I can do that. I can make risks easier and not so risky."

"Right! That's what they all say, but here in the Valley of Comfort, things are comfortable," Morgan continued, "and mediocre. Take a look over here, behind me."

Erik peered over her shoulder and saw an office crowded with people, but, strangely, it looked more like something out of the

1950s or '60s. There was no new technology in sight that would help increase everyone's productivity.

"So change must be difficult to achieve here," he said.

Harry laughed. "Difficult? These people are so engrossed in their comfort zones, they don't see beyond their next coffee break. Not only do they not embrace new technology, when it comes to new trends, they can't see beyond their noses," he explained. "Short answer, change is darned near impossible in this place."

"We call it the 'Super Glue effect.' These people couldn't change, couldn't escape from their comfort zones, even if you handed them a stick of dynamite," Al offered, sadly shaking his head.

"Caroline's been the manager here for quite a while and when you say the manager is the glue ... ol' Caroline here qualifies as Super Glue. Back several years ago, she decided that installing new accounting software would just put too much strain on her employees. She couldn't quite grasp the concept herself, so she thought having to learn the new software would stress her people. Besides, everyone was so comfortable with their old accounting system that technology passed them by," Morgan pointed out.

"Here's another thing. Take a look at this folder of performance reviews," Al suggested.

"They all look the same," Erik observed. In fact, the difference between the best review and the lowest review is less than a point. Check this out. The wording is the same on every review. This whole team must be exactly the same or Caroline just changes the names and gives the same review to everyone. It doesn't take much courage to tell everyone they are all great − even when they are not doing their jobs. No wonder they've found this comfort zone, and are now stuck."

"Here's another thing that blows my mind." Morgan went on. "The employees treat their customers the way they are treated. By the time they hear from their customers, they've not only lost current business but future customers as well. You can see that there's really not much emphasis on response time because no one is aware that this keeps customers happy. There's little room for individual innovation or superior customer service because that, of course, would be way out of range for all of them."

Erik made a motion to move along, but Harry's strong hand stopped him in his tracks. "Wait, there's more. Caroline is also good at ignoring problems such as her team's inability to respond in a timely manner. They need technology to be able to compete," Harry explained.

"Yeah, but Caroline thought the problem would take care of itself, so she decided to do exactly nothing, which is what she did," Jason added. "Today, except for a few loyal friends, the customer list has been decimated."

"So, addressing the little problem of improving response time would have headed off what is now a huge issue," Erik said, shaking his head. "But, are all these employees comfortable in their mediocrity?"

"The answer is a resounding 'yes!'" Morgan said, turning to confront Erik. "In the Valley of Comfort there's no creativity in solving problems. They don't take the time to listen to or give positive recognition to their customers. Their customers are waiting in the Customer's Cave of Apathy – waiting to find another company to take their business. Can you blame them?"

"Who is that over there?" Erik wondered.

"Who?" Angela asked.

"That guy running around with that long piece of paper? I've been watching him, and he's come close to stumbling over that monster several times."

Angela looked in the direction that Erik was pointing. "Oh, him. I really don't know his name. We just call him 'Wish List Wally.'"

"That's an interesting name. Kind of clever, in fact," Erik said, smiling. "But what in the heck is he doing?"

"His entire job is to monitor and maintain the office wish list ... and that long piece of paper is what everybody keeps hoping will happen," Angela said, shaking her head. "Unfortunately, nobody has any goals leading up to the items on the wish list, such as better customer communications, higher product visibility, better customer service or streamlined processes. And, there is no accountability to make them happen. No, everybody just talks about what they wish they could accomplish, and Wally writes it down on the list."

"Sounds like another road to nowhere, another treadmill like the one we saw back at the cave," replied Erik. "What a waste."

Just then, one of the workers waved frantically.

"Who is the woman standing on her desk, waving the white hanky?" asked Erik.

"Oh, that's Anne," Morgan said. "She's been trying to get out of this valley for years now, but every time she tries something new, her manager moves her back to square one."

"And Anne doesn't mind?"

"Most of the people who work here think this is the absolute perfect place to work, except Anne and maybe a few others," Morgan said. "Look at their smiling faces. They really believe they've made it to the best possible place. However, if you take a closer look, you'll find out there's not one person in this valley who has grown in the past two years. All of them have the same exact skills they came with."

"Oh, so that's why it's so crowded," Erik observed.

"Right you are. It's easy to get into the Valley of Comfort but very difficult to get out. People really like it here … and whenever someone with a lot of talent – like Anne – tries to get out, the others work like the devil to keep them here. It's more comfortable, keeping everybody together at one pace, although they're going nowhere," Morgan explained.

"Yeah, sort of like misery loves company," Erik said under his breath. "Your choice of words – work like the devil, for example – really says it all, doesn't it?"

"There's something else about that office that's not obvious to the first-time visitor," Harry pointed out. "Caroline, their manager, doesn't want to make anyone uncomfortable, so everyone either gets recognized the same or not at all. That's the way it's always been … so people on the team aren't focused on anything but their own comfort zones. No, they don't try anything new … why should they? There's no incentive to move the organization to the next level. The best people eventually grow frustrated and often leave the company or transfer to the Apathy Cave."

"And besides, it might not be as comfortable as it is for them all right now," Angela added.

"Man, it doesn't smell as musty and people don't seem to be languishing here like they were back in Apathy Cave, but this place is equally lethal, especially when it comes to individual potential," Erik said as he shook his head. "What a waste of ability, and what a bland future for these folks."

"Absolutely," Jason agreed. "And don't let your eyes deceive you. These people and this team are headed for the cave. It's only a matter of time."

"Right, buddy. On track and nearing their destination. Heading for the last roundup," said Al. "They don't look it and they don't know it, but they're dying on the vine here. And Apathy Cave is just around the corner in their future because they're not getting anything done. But one thing's certain: They're all comfortable. They are never asked – or permitted – to take risks, and they like working here. But, like that clear pond in the nice warm sun, it will soon turn into a stagnant cesspool if there is no movement and fresh oxygen."

"I'd like it, too," Morgan laughed, "if I were a zombie-in-training."

"So, where do the new ideas go?" asked Erik. "What do people do about their personal goals and ambitions? Where's all the energy?"

"Aren't any," Harry said, simply. "If there were new ideas, new goals and new vision, they would all fall into the 'take-a-risk' category, and nobody here is up to doing that. Why should they when they're so comfortable and life is so easy … according to them?"

"But why?" asked Erik.

"Maybe because management has discouraged it," was Morgan's answer. "Maybe because Caroline, the manager, didn't want anyone to be a superstar, so her main focus is to make everyone mediocre. And she's done an excellent job of that."

Erik noticed a few of the workers were ashen and pale, like those he had seen back in the cave. "Who are those people?" he wanted to know.

Jason looked closely. "They look like some fugitives from the cave," he said matter-of-factly, "but that's the thing about the Valley of Comfort. Some of the team members eventually escape Apathy Cave, particularly when Bruce takes one of his two- or three-hour lunches, which is his usual routine these days.

"Anyway, they escape that dead zone but only get as far as this valley," Jason explained, "and things are so comfortable here, particularly when you compare it to where they've been, they have the same reaction you had before you knew anything about it. They think they've found paradise."

"Sounds pretty grim," Erik agreed. "But, is Management Land all this grim? I mean, isn't there an upside?"

"You'll have to make that decision after we finish our tour," Al said. "I'll agree, things are pretty grim here, but think about how we all felt when these managers showed up to lead our team. There were times when giving blood would have been preferable to working with them."

"I'll second that motion," Angela piped in. "Erik, put yourself in our place. We were jazzed about getting a new manager, hoping for the best but always ending up with people like Bruce and Caroline. We had all this talent but felt like we were treading water the whole time.

"Admittedly, we did lose a few people along the way, people who were excellent team members and perfect matches to our talent pool, but that's water under the bridge now."

"I don't think I can really feel what you guys were feeling because I wasn't there with you, but I'd bet you were not only frustrated but often discouraged and ready to give up," Erik said.

"And that's putting it mildly," Harry said. "After Caroline's warm and fuzzy meetings, I'd want to slit my wrists and bleed to death rather than go through one more of those feel-good exercises. To put it bluntly, there was never any meat in those meetings. We learned things in the schools we went to, but implementing new ideas or new programs? Simply out of the question. According to Caroline, the changes might make someone uncomfortable."

"Okay, okay. I'm getting the picture, loud and clear. So can we move on to our next stop, please?" Erik begged. "This comfortable valley is beginning to get to me. Looking under the rug and finding so much awful stuff is giving me the creeps … like opening a cabinet in our first apartment and finding it filled with insects. And this place isn't even half as bad as the cave."

"Okay, we need to get going anyway," Morgan agreed. "We have another couple of stops before we have to get back."

As the group marched on, Erik took a look over his shoulder. "Comfort Valley, with all of its tranquility and calm, wasn't so comfortable after all," he thought as he hiked on. "Like poor frogs in a pot of water, and someone's turning up the heat, just a little at a time, until the water's boiling."

THE VALLEY OF COMFORT

SYMPTOMS

- Easy to get there. Hard to leave.
- Most natural place to be. Very close to human nature.
- Average employees are happy, but they don't know anything different.
- Comfortable – avoid risks at all costs.
- Frustrating place for high-achievers.
- Every effort is mediocre. Greatest enemy to individual potential.
- Don't see things coming. No vision for the future.
- Few, if any meetings or planning sessions focus on the *what-ifs* or change for the better. Never challenge the status quo.
- When asked, few can tell you what the main thing is.

EXIT STRATEGIES

- Connect with your team and identify personal and professional goals and passions, individual strengths and developmental opportunities, reward and recognition needs.
- Commit to personal development for your team, providing ongoing learning opportunities.
- Create a climate that allows and encourages risks.
- Recognize and reward success based on each individual's values and motivators.
- Encourage new ideas to be discussed by asking your team, "What are we missing if we take off all the parameters and eliminate all the barriers?" This will open up free thinking.

"The man whose life is devoted to paperwork has lost the initiative.
He is dealing with things that are brought to his notice,
having ceased to notice anything for himself."
– N.C. Parkinson, English Writer

Only minutes later, as the group began walking through a rather dark and forested part of the landscape, Erik suddenly heard a deep gurgling noise. The air around him grew thick with humidity and he stopped for a moment to wipe his brow with the handkerchief he always carried in his pocket.

"What's that noise up ahead?" he asked as he replaced the hanky and trotted to catch up with the rest of his team. "Please don't let it be the Molehill of the Monsters," he quipped lamely.

"Oh, that noise?" Harry said, rather unassumingly. "No, it is not a molehill. What you hear is the sounds of a swamp and a carousel."

"Yeah, the swamp. Be careful where you step," Jason advised. "It's easy to sink around here. We've lost count of how many people have come here and were never seen again."

"Is that your plan for me?" Erik managed another weak laugh.

"You've got to start trusting us," Harry said, clapping him on the shoulder as he passed Erik, who had taken off his ball cap and folded it into his back pocket.

"Well, maybe you better tell me about the swamp … and the carousel," suggested Erik. "Remember, I have a wife and kids at home, and they're relying on me for medical insurance."

Morgan laughed. "I suppose we should tell you."

"Let me tell him," Angela chimed in, her usual happy-go-lucky smile fading from her face.

"I'm listening," said Erik, stopping on the trail to again wipe the moisture from his face.

"It's the Paperwork Swamp and the E-mail Carousel," Angela began, "and it is a place in Management Land where unimportant things control important time."

"Let me take it from here," Harry said. "You've never seen the Paperwork Swamp before, but you've probably seen how they begin, because, sadly, they're so prevalent. They literally dot our business landscape, and most people are so accustomed to working in the Paperwork Swamp that they just take it for granted. I mean, they expect their workplace to look this way."

Erik nodded. "I know all about paperwork. It's been an ongoing battle in my career. And what about the carousel?"

"It's something that, once you get on, you can't get off," Morgan offered. "It's the CCs, the BCCs and the interminable responses that steal your time until there's nothing left."

"It's that eerie tone that tells you another e-mail has arrived," Harry added, "the tone that – like the effect the bell had on Pavlov's dogs – causes you to turn away from all other priorities so you can open the e-mail, read it, distribute it, copy in management and then CC everyone on your team."

Shaking his head, Erik began to visualize the entire scenario up ahead. "I remember one of my own managers who spent so much time with the CCs, the BCCs and the CYAs that he literally never came out of his office. So the carousel keeps going and going, and you can never get off unless you jump."

"And then you end up in Paperwork Swamp," Harry said, his face expressionless at this point.

"It's the same for all of us," Morgan agreed. "What makes this particular swamp unique is that it's the worst-case scenario. Remember reading *Dante's Divine Comedy* where the entrance to Hades was marked with a sign reading, 'Abandon hope, all ye who enter here'?"

"Vaguely. Although I only had one course in European literature."

"Well, that's the same sign you'll find at the entrance of the Paperwork Swamp," Morgan continued. "It's a dismal place, a place where people – including their leader – are hopeless slaves to paperwork. In fact, no one has proved this, but we think these employees actually eat paper because they seem to be addicted to having it around all of the time."

As the group approached, the humidity continued to rise, the billowing steam rose from the murky swamp as far as the eye could see and the eerie calliope of the e-mail carousel puffed out each gruesome note.

"There's poor Kevin over there. He was always the most conscientious about getting paperwork accomplished," Jason pointed out. "Even stayed late and worked weekends to get every last scrap filed before deadlines."

"I remember Kevin," Erik said, scanning the horizon, hoping to see the young graduate who had started his career with the company. "He was bright, I mean really bright," he recalled.

"He was always making new files and then neatly filing each project alphabetically in his desk," Morgan added.

"Kevin was strictly by the book," Harry commented. "Finally, one day the stacks of paperwork totally overwhelmed him and pushed him into the swamp. Here, he's one of the lucky ones because he has managed to keep his head above the surface, but periodic surges – like month-end reports – sometimes cause him to spend time submerged. Notice, his fingers are beginning to web. Poor guy probably hasn't seen his feet since he got here."

About that time, Morgan waved to a younger woman who had come slogging through the middle of the swamp.

"You know her?" asked Erik.

"That's Contingency Connie. She came in with great credentials."

"So, why is she here?"

"Connie is a four-spare-tire-person," Morgan began. "She's always worrying about something happening, so she keeps busy focusing on making sure she has Plan B and C in place. Sadly, that keeps her from focusing on the program or process at hand."

"Four-spare-tire-person? I don't understand," Erik said.

"Connie owns one of the finest automobiles in the company parking lot. But, she's so concerned about the possibility of something bad happening to her car, she has loaded her trunk full of tools and spare parts. The rumor is that she has four spare tires just in case all four tires go flat at once," Morgan explained.

"Oh, I know the type. On one family vacation, my father-in-law was so busy loading the car with extra fan belts, extra oil, tools and engine coolant, he forgot to load his wife's suitcase. She never let him hear the end of it."

"That's Connie. Lots of talent, but she always over thinks her job and, as a result, under-delivers. Contingency plans are important, but there comes a time when you need to make a decision to do something besides make plans."

"But, where are the managers?" Erik wondered out loud. "Can't they direct her to do something instead of making contingency plans all day?"

"Manager, manager," Angela repeated, looking around. "Oh, there's one over there – Dick Perlman. Actually, he was never a very good manager, but he could generate the paper like nobody in the business. When he was with our group, we decided Dick came up with new paperwork processes to convince senior management he was doing something productive. But all he actually did was kill our productivity. "The other thing about Perlman is, well, he's addicted."

"Addicted to what?" Erik wanted to know.

"He's addicted to technology," Angela explained. "He spends more time tinkering with his personal organizer, PowerPoints™, sending e-mails, and playing with new programs than he spends actually talking to his troops. He's never available, so most of his team has to be content speaking to his voice mail. If they've got a question, they get better results sending an e-mail than walking down the hall to his office and talking over a problem."

"Sadly," Jason pointed out, "Perlman was more in touch with his paperwork than his people."

"What do you mean?" asked Erik.

"He was always focused on his processes and paperwork. He never bothered to get to know any of us. I'll bet if you put a gun to his head and asked him anything about us today – like where we went to school or if we were married or what our partners' names were – he couldn't tell you. Even if his life depended on it."

"It was almost like he was hiding behind the paper and technology so he wouldn't have to get to know us," Morgan agreed. "Only, in his arm's-length approach, he also missed out on learning our true talents and where those could be plugged in to move our team ahead of the curve.

"He was so busy generating paperwork that he failed to pay attention to his team. He never listened to their comments, never heeded their concerns or offered suggestions when they needed help. The paper shuffling actually edged out any room for employee input, conferences or work sessions."

"So the noise I was hearing wasn't human," Erik reasoned. "It was the sound of paper being copied, circulated, stamped, stapled, filed and stacked."

"That's true. He was totally oblivious to his team," Al said. "Instead of simplifying things, he made everything more complex."

Erik, still wiping the humidity from his face, slumped against a stump and surveyed the swamp, shaking his head. Paper. Loads of paper stacked everywhere. Workers slogged from station to station, getting paperwork stamped, circulating paperwork for signatures and one even carried a "read" file that was thicker than any dictionary. Still others spent the day going through e-mail after e-mail, deleting some and forwarding others – a vicious circle, just like a carousel.

Wizen and bent workers struggled under the sheer weight of stacks of paper. As the humidity slowly circulated through the swamp, much of the paper began to transform into illegible, sticky glop, like a vast ocean of papier-mâché. Except nothing artistic would be done with it. It merely pulled workers deeper into the muck that was rising to their desktops.

"But here's the real danger this swamp holds," said Morgan, after a few moments, her expression more serious than ever. "When you work in a paperwork swamp, you'll soon find yourself caught up in a whirlpool of excuses. This is where excuses are born, hatched and, if you'll look closely, you'll see lots of little excuses swirling under this bridge we're standing on. Over toward the swamp's main tributary, the excuses are bigger and impact many more people."

Erik looked closely. Sure enough, there were excuses like, "I didn't take action because I never received your response." Another excuse claimed, "I didn't receive your order in time, so the shipment will be late." Still another, "I didn't make it to the meeting because I didn't get the memo." Every good idea was met with more paperwork to justify trying anything new. People in the swamp finally realized that they were being punished for being creative – the paperwork swamp was killing ideas.

"Man, I never knew there were so many excuses before, except some of these sound strangely familiar," commented Erik.

"You'll find excuses for everything here, from late reports to poor performance and from missed business to customers you'll never see again," Harry explained. "All because paperwork became the one thing – the only thing – these people focused on."

"Did all this confusion affect your morale?" Erik asked, his expression matching the seriousness of Morgan's.

"Did it ever! Before the manager was finally sucked into the whirlpool of year-end paperwork, he had killed our group's productivity, not to mention the spirit of our team," Morgan said. "Because he had failed to maintain focus, we were all wandering aimlessly about in our careers, trying to figure out what was happening to our business and never getting any answers. Just more paperwork. The irony of the paperwork swamp is that the more paperwork you create, the more secure you feel in the swamp. Most of the time without even knowing it."

Erik nodded sympathetically. "So, you don't want a repeat performance?"

"That's an understatement, my friend," Al responded. "We all bring a wide variety of talents to the table, and we don't want them buried with more paperwork or endless e-mails," he added.

"I can see how that could happen," Erik answered. "Just look at poor Kevin. He was a real up-and-comer, I remember. Now he's just dealing with mountains of paperwork, and he seems to be smiling."

"Don't be fooled," Morgan warned. "If you listen closely, you'll also hear Kevin making excuses," Jason noted. "That's why he's going to end up in the cave, just like everyone else who spends too much time in Management Land. He's got an excuse for everything, including the reason he never took the initiative to stop filling out every form and written request that landed on his desk."

"Poor guy. His future isn't very bright here in the swamp, and I don't know how any of the workers can even function with all this humidity," Erik pointed out, noticing algae growing on the toes of his sneakers.

"Well, they've got an excuse for the weather around here, too. They move slowly on everything and say it's because they didn't get the memo on how to regulate the thermostat," Jason said, trying not to smile. "It's a Catch-22 with a never-ending cycle of paper and e-mail."

"I just have one question," Erik said, standing and dusting the fine white dust from the swamp's bubbling broth from his jeans. "Even though some managers commit overkill with paperwork, how do you know when your team is overloaded?"

"Leaders listen, while most managers are content to assume," Angela volunteered. "If you have a question about paperwork overload, too many hours demanded by a certain project or not enough challenge for certain employees, just ask. That's what we're here to do … to give leaders our input so they can make good decisions about how we can best use our time to meet corporate goals."

"Sounds like the best way to sort things out," Erik agreed.

"It all goes back to basic communication, beyond handheld communication devices, e-mails and voice links," Jason continued. "If you look on the carousel, you'll see entire teams, trying to answer e-mails on their handheld systems. And when there are no e-mails to answer, they'll e-mail each other. Having one more e-mail to them is like job security."

"So, what should their manager do? Take their handhelds away?" Erik wanted to know.

"The best thing that manager could do would be to take time, periodically, to take the group's pulse," Jason suggested. "That would head off these no-brainer activities that usurp time from what their real focus should be. Just taking time to ask how members of the team are spending most of their time would pay dividends like you wouldn't believe. Plus, it would give everyone a feeling of being of value and making a contribution to the team rather than taking care of housekeeping chores all day."

"Okay, okay … once again, you've done an excellent job of making your point," Erik relented, "and I promise to do everything in my power to keep the paperwork – and the e-mails – to the necessary minimums. But I wonder if you would want to include paperwork, such as processing the paperwork for bonuses."

"Well, there are some things we'll make an exception for," Morgan said. Then the group broke into laughter.

"We're flexible where that kind of paperwork is involved," Jason joked as the group left the hot, humid Swamp of Paperwork, heading for higher elevations. Elevations that Erik hoped would be cool enough to dry out his still-moist clothing.

Paperwork Swamp

Symptoms

- Endless reports, never-ending strings of e-mail responses and excessive conference calls.
- Focus is on unimportant activities. Important deadlines are missed.
- Management emphasis is on looking in the "rear view mirror," always dwelling on the past and ensuring the completion of paperwork. The focus is rarely on the future.
- Team is working hard and achieving little. Busy people producing mediocre performance.
- Addiction to technology and avoidance of personal connections.
- No clear definition of what is important.

Exit Strategies

- Conduct a personal paperwork audit for one week. Identify what you respond to, what you create or require. Then set a goal to reduce that by 25 percent.
- Clearly identify the key activities to your success, then focus on those activities.
- Turn the team's efforts toward achieving results, not documenting the process.
- Communicate with upper management, letting them know what they're doing to slow progress with paperwork jams and providing suggestions to eliminate unnecessary reports and meetings.
- Ask your team: "What paperwork and current policies and procedures are barriers to performance?" Review the list and eliminate paper and outdated policies where possible.

FOURTH STOP:
PANIC PEAK

*"Panic is a thin stream of fear trickling through the mind.
If encouraged, it cuts a channel into which all other thoughts are drained."*
– Robert Albert Bloch, Writer

Another short, 15-minute walk left the Paperwork Swamp well behind the group, but Erik was still reeling from what he had seen. "I wonder," he thought, "how easy it would be for an entire team to fall into the swamp, never to be seen again?"

His thoughts were suddenly interrupted by an unusual sound. As the group gained elevation, they could discern voices, many voices. Some were screaming unintelligible orders. Others were asking for help. "Who is that and what are they saying? Do they need help?" he asked Harry, who had been walking slightly behind him and seemed not to hear the noise that was growing louder with every step forward.

"That, my friend means we're nearing Panic Peak," Harry said, seemingly unconcerned as the din grew even louder.

Climbing slightly higher, the air became thick and foggy with confusion and frustration. Either the increasing altitude or this unusually dense fog made it more and more difficult to breathe. "Is it much farther?" Erik panted, gasping for every painful breath.

"Just a few more steps," Morgan assured him.

Erik thought it was strange. None of the group seemed intimidated by the continual lowering of visibility.

By the time they reached the summit, the roar was deafening and the fog was thicker. People darting in every direction made it difficult for the group to stay together.

Erik found himself alone in the mob, surrounded by people who were running, shouting and looking dismayed. In a few moments, Jason was by his side and tapping him on the shoulder. "Welcome to Panic Peak," Jason shouted in his ear. "Sooo … what do you think?"

"Man, I think this is worse than bedlam," Erik said, his eyes wide as he strained to take in the sight before him. "Is this the loony bin or what?"

Jason chuckled. "Well, that's definitely what it looks like, but no, most of these people are totally sane. The problem is there is no direction or vision. There are no rules or discipline in Panic Peak. You can do anything you want as long as you are busy."

Erik nodded. "Oh, are those the only problems?"

By this time, Morgan had joined the two men. "Here's our ride. Hop in."

"But where are we going?" Erik asked.

"It's our own private guided tour. We'll see some incredible sights along the way," she continued.

At that moment, the van lurched to a stop as the driver listened to the dispatcher. "Go ahead to Pilot Point," a voice squawked through the speaker.

With those directions, the driver sharply turned the van to the right and began a slow ascent up a road that snaked along the mountain's rim. After several miles, the van lurched to another stop. "Forget Pilot Point. Take your passengers to Consternation Crest," the dispatcher shouted. "They needed to be there 10 minutes ago!"

"Ten-four," said the driver, wheeling the van back down the road until they reached a crossroads and he guided the van back to the left. Five minutes down a ruggedly bumpy road, the speaker squawked more directions. "Take your passengers back to the embarcadero," it instructed.

By this time, Erik was beginning to feel dizzy from riding in the back seat and the constant lurching of the van's stops and starts. "What's the problem?" he asked Harry, who was seated to his left.

"It's common around here. In all the confusion, there's no clear vision and, definitely no direction. We've been on this trip with managers many times before. As soon as we're clear about one mission and vision, the manager changes direction for the team and we're left not making any headway at all," Harry explained. "For a good example, just look out the window and figure our mileage for being in this van for more than a half-hour."

Erik glanced at his watch and then looked out the window. "Why, isn't this the place we started our tour?"

"Exactly," Angela nodded. "This is the wildest of goose chases, but we've spent hours of our valuable time heading in one direction only to have our manager suddenly change focus and take us down a totally different road."

As the riders piled out of the van to nowhere, Morgan caught Erik looking at the scene ahead of him and frowning. "Oh, the people here aren't bad people," she explained. "They are here because, at least, they care enough not to be in Apathy Cave and they are not satisfied to be in the Valley of Comfort, either."

"That quick tour we just took is a clear illustration of how work doesn't move forward," Jason added.

Erik nodded knowingly. "Let me guess. Here in Panic Peak the managers give directions, then they change course, mid-project, just like the dispatcher. Am I right?"

Harry suddenly appeared at Erik's side. "I'd like to show you a good example of who works here," he said. "Follow me."

The two men stopped, some distance away from a worker who was busily hanging banners and posters around the office. "What's his job?" Erik wanted to know.

"That's Benjamin. His job – his only job – is to continually change the program of the month here," Harry said. "Except the programs never really last a month, and by the time workers realize they should be focusing on something else, it's time for another program change."

"I think I know what you mean," Erik nodded. "A couple of years ago, there was a real push for everyone to cut expenses, and as soon as we were all on track to make that happen, somebody decided our real focus should be on customer service. Then, safety was made our number one priority, until we were on deadline with a big project. Then safety faded out of the picture and exceeding customer expectations became our next big focus."

"Single-handedly, that one guy and his new programs keep people in a panic around here," Harry concluded.

"I can see why," Erik agreed.

"Look at Joe over there," Morgan shouted, pointing to a younger man with a pocket full of pens and notebooks under both arms. "He works 15 hours a day, but management's changing priorities. Their inability to provide strong leadership is paving the way for poor Joe to end up in the cave within a few short months. In fact, most of the people you saw in Apathy Cave are willing transfers from Panic Peak."

"You mean they'd rather be there than here?" Erik was speechless as he took a closer look at the people residing in this third stop on his tour of Management Land. He saw groups meeting, and then re-meeting, to talk about the same topic. Managers held meetings for hours and no decisions were made. Then, when a decision emerged, memo after memo was generated – each providing workers with a different set of directives.

Activities were occurring everywhere, but none were productive. Training was followed by retraining, but as management's focus changed, much of the training was irrelevant to the team's mission. In one craggy corner of the peak, workers were running in circles, as if one shoe was bolted to the floor. Upon taking a closer look, Erik found that was exactly the case. And some of the cries he had heard coming up the mountain were cries from these people, wanting someone to rescue them from their dizzying paths.

Ultimately, he learned, many of the people on Panic Peak were scurrying, trying to find busy work to fill their workday, sandwiched between extended breaks to give them relief from the constant roar and the chaos that greeted them, week in and week out.

"As you can see," shouted Al, pushing his way through the tumult to join his group, "a lot of decisions are being made here and a lot of activities are under way, but the best decisions and the most productive activities don't come from this part of Management Land."

"But why? How?" Erik wanted to know.

"If a manager creates confusion, the team will live in confusion," Al said. "It's really that simple. The manager sets the tone, and if that manager is not organized and thoroughly involved in the company or team's vision, chaos is an easy result."

"But, making a decision isn't that difficult," Erik said. "Why should it be such a big problem here?"

"Probably because much of what you're seeing are directions that actually contradict each other," Angela pointed out. "Plus, look over there. See that large contraption?"

Erik nodded.

"It's grown larger even since our last visit. It runs 24 hours a day and has an endless supply of energy. It's called 'the rumor mill' and, of course, that adds to the panic and chaos around this place," she continued. "It's also one reason for the huge amount of stress around here."

All Erik could do was shake his head.

"This is also the training ground for the world's best code-talkers," Jason yelled into Erik's ear.

"Code-talker? What's that?"

"When managers can't lead and can't express their ideas or expectations, they often speak in code," Jason responded. "Like, when the boss says, 'You take care of it' and he or she really means, 'Do the project, but do it exactly as I outlined, and be sure to follow up with me after every step.'"

Morgan added. "We get mixed signals, mixed messages and pretty soon it mixes us up so we don't really know what they mean. Sometimes they just say 'take care of it' and we are expected to know exactly the definition of what it is and how to take care of it."

"Oh, I get it." Erik said. "Yep, I've had managers like that myself. When she said, 'Take care of it,' I knew I had better get really good at reading her mind or I'd get called in for even the tiniest step I took outside her rigid guidelines. But I guess we all have those experiences."

"And that's why we brought you to Management Land in the first place," Morgan continued. "Because we're tired of the chaos, confusion, lack of direction and every other problem you've seen so far today."

As Erik struggled to make his way through wave after wave of panicked employees who were rushing around aimlessly, like so many charged ions in an atom, he saw some people burst through the doors in a panic. They cowered at their desks, afraid to make eye contact.

"See that guy with the blue shirt and red tie?" Angela asked. "That's Bryan. He's Harvard Business. Really bright. Lots of dynamic energy and great ideas. He came here with all the right stuff."

"You mean the guy with the funky glasses and pale skin who just crawled under his desk?"

"Yep, that's him. He's searching for the vision he lost after being on Panic Peak less than a week. His 'funky glasses' as you called them are really blinders. He's also insecure; it's going to take some couch time to bring him back to where he could appreciate his full potential. In the meantime, the changes of direction, the lack of direction and the overall confusion have just about driven him over the edge."

"How could this happen?" he asked.

"Easy," Harry replied. "Every worker you see is reacting to an assignment or an issue without a clear vision. Remember, we told you every site on this Land is reactive. Well, now you can see what we mean.

"Then too, as you may know, some managers absolutely thrive on chaos," Harry continued. "In fact, they wouldn't want to work any place else. And if things started to go smoothly around here, they'd start behaving in such a way to create their own chaos and confusion. If the manager creates that kind of environment, the team has to learn to live in that chaos."

"One of our managers was exactly as Harry describes him," Angela affirmed. "We were all ready to hand in our resignations by the time we figured him out and started directing ourselves. Well, he couldn't stand the order and methodical approach we developed, so he left."

"And you were happy?" Erik wondered.

"Ecstatic!" Morgan beamed. "Some of us were beginning to doubt ourselves, our abilities and our own sanity. Our office was in a state of total paranoia. Needless to say, it was really tough coming to work every day."

"You can say that again," Al said, trying to stay out of the path of the workers' chaotic onslaught. "Our group was focused, self-assured and ultra-productive before the new boss brought his chaos and confusion to our team. By the time he left, we were frustrated, stressed to the max and, in some cases, desperate."

"Desperate?"

"Absolutely, and in more ways than one. Our boss didn't lay any groundwork for trust in our team, so we all ended up pretty paranoid … about everything. And desperate! Desperate to achieve, to see our careers progress," Al explained. "Every time we took a step forward in one direction, our manager would change directions and, sometimes, even our mission. Then we were back at square one, not knowing if we had succeeded or failed, not knowing even if we would have a job the next day. We could all see we were going nowhere but were helpless to do anything because of the leadership – or lack of it – that our team was getting."

"It was like having momentum and the desire to move ahead but being attached to a rubber band. So every time we made progress, we would be jerked backward," Harry remembered. "It was a nightmare."

By this time, Erik was covering his ears and dodging the bodies hurtling past him as their panic and the continuing chaos catapulted them from one place to another. "Can we go? Can we please go," he pleaded. "My head is splitting and, believe me, I've gotten the message."

The team looked at each other and then Morgan spoke. "Well, we still have one stop to make, but it will be up to you, whether or not we get there."

And for the umpteenth time that day, Erik was puzzled. "Up to me?"

"Exactly," Jason responded. "If you answer three questions correctly, we will actually be leaving Management Land and crossing the bridge to Leader Land. It's right across the channel, but they don't let just anybody in. And they'll only let us pass if your responses to the three questions are acceptable to the bridge masters."

"Bridge masters?"

"The bridge masters to Leader Land are all veteran leaders. You'll notice each has their share of battle scars. That's because they've all spent time in every area of Management Land but always returned to Leader Land. Their mission is to only allow managers with strong leadership potential to transition to Leader Land.

Erik was always up for a challenge. In fact, he had been known for being daring and a risk-taker. "Okay, let's hear those questions. I'm ready. After these experiences today, I think I may be ready for anything – and afraid of nothing."

PANIC PEAK

SYMPTOMS

♦ Confusion and paranoia create the tone every day.

♦ Employees are stressed, frustrated and insecure.

♦ Leaders constantly change direction. Decisions are made and then changed.

♦ Best decisions are not made here.

♦ People are paranoid and rumors are rampant.

♦ "Programs" of the month come and go with regularity.

EXIT STRATEGIES

♦ Identify, clarify and solidify the main thing. Don't merely communicate "the main thing" to your team. Connect them to "the main thing."

♦ Ask each member of your team these two simple but powerful questions: 1. What are two activities we are doing today that we should stop doing to increase our productivity and effectiveness? 2. What am I, as your manager, or what is the organization doing that causes confusion in our work group?

♦ Develop plans to eliminate confusion and those activities that are barriers to productivity and effectiveness.

♦ Minimize strategy changes.

♦ Conduct coaching sessions with team members, focusing on goals, goal attainment, clear roles and milestones to ensure forward progress and continuous feedback.

FIFTH STOP:
LEADER LAND

*"True leadership must be for the benefit of the followers,
not the enrichment of the leader."*
– Robert Townsend

After quickly descending the fog, the gloom and the chaos of Panic Peak, the group followed a well-manicured path for several miles until they came to the azure waters spanned by the suspension bridge to Leader Land.

"This is the Bridge of Learning and Connection," Harry announced as the group neared the impressive structure, gleaming in the late afternoon sun. "This is how we can escape Management Land, Erik, and this is where your test begins," he added.

As Erik shaded his eyes and looked toward the bridge, he could see three separate checkpoints and a uniformed bridge master standing at each. "But, I want to be a manager. I want to manage the team."

Morgan offered him a cold bottle of water. "You still don't get it, do you?" she asked. "Here, stop and take a drink before we start across."

"Yeah, you might want to sit and rest for a moment before you attempt crossing," Al counseled. "It may be tough getting across."

"I have confidence in you, Erik," Morgan announced as she sat down on a trailside log. "I've been watching his reactions closely during the tour and I think he may have no trouble passing each of the checkpoints."

"But, what if I don't want to leave?" Erik protested again. "I'm committed to be the best manager you've ever had."

"What you need to understand is that we don't want to be managed," Al said, his usually quiet voice remaining calm as he provided an explanation. What we want is for you to be our leader and our coach. We want you to provide us with direction, serve as a confidante when we need one and respect us when we have something to contribute."

"Yeah," Jason stepped forward. "What you need to understand, particularly after taking this tour, is that you, as our leader, influence our career paths and our futures more than anything or anybody else in the organization. You create an environment of trust. You set the tone for everything we do. So, we want you to be our leader. And we want to work together to make our team stronger, more efficient and more effective than we've ever been."

"That's exactly what we want," Harry agreed. "Remember, we've had other managers. We all tried to be positive and think the best when the last four managers came in, and look where it got us!"

"But we didn't bother to bring them here first," Angela pointed out. "Maybe if we'd given each of them the tour, they would have tried harder to prevent themselves from ending up here."

"So, when a manager fails, they end up in Management Land?" asked Erik.

"Not all of them," Harry explained. "Some find other work, but many of those who decide to stay in management eventually end up here."

Erik thought for a moment. He couldn't picture himself surviving Apathy Cave, much less the Valley of Comfort, Paperwork Swamp or Panic Peak. "Then I'd better learn how to be the best leader I can be," he said to himself, trying to remember what he had learned from his favorite mentors and his college management professors.

"Remember, you've got responsibilities at home," Angela said, smiling. "People there are depending on you, and so are we. But we all know you can succeed."

Taking a deep breath, the new manager rose to his feet, dusted himself off and pronounced himself ready to escape Management Land and cross the bridge to Leader Land. "Okay, show me the way," he said. "I'm ready."

When the group reached the first checkpoint, the bridge master – a wizen man with white hair and a long beard stepped out of the adjacent guardhouse. "Aha! Another candidate," he exclaimed. "Looks fairly bright, but so did many of those I failed," he said, stroking the mustache that melted into his beard. "Well, we'll see," he said to no one in particular. "We'll see."

Erik stood straighter, as if addressing a commanding officer. "I'm ready. Anytime you are, sir."

The bridge master looked at him and squinted. "First, I want these other folks to step away from you. I've had some groups who wanted to help their managers with the answers and that's not how we operate here."

Obediently, the group stepped back several steps, leaving Erik to face the bridge master alone.

"My question is this," the older man said slowly. "What are your goals for your team?"

Erik thought several moments before speaking, carefully organizing his thoughts. Then he cleared his voice. "My answer is this: My goal for my team is to help each member develop to his or her full potential. I realize no two team members will have the same personal goals or the same strengths. So my priority is to provide them with the tools they'll need to individually realize their goals while exploring and strengthening their passions and their abilities. And then, I'll be there to coach them."

As Erik provided his answer, the old man studied his boots, well scuffed from years of hard wear. "So, that's what you have to say for yourself, is it?" he said, finally looking up at Erik with his steely stare.

"Yes, yes, sir," Erik responded, not able to determine from the older man's expression if his answer had been acceptable or not."

"And you sincerely believe that's your role as a manager?" the bridge master asked.

"With all the sincerity I have," said Erik. "I see coaching my team to be the best they can be as a high priority."

Meanwhile, the group – obviously impressed with what Erik had said – was beaming and nodding to each other knowing that Erik truly cared about them and their futures as well as his own.

"Well, young man. You're cleared to the next checkpoint. Congratulations!" the bridge master said, and as he swung open the gate, the group standing behind Erik cheered.

"Way to go," Harry said.

"Good answer," Morgan agreed.

As the ensemble passed the first checkpoint, Angela appeared at Erik's side. "The next question will be a little tougher, but don't worry. You're doing great," she said, trying to encourage him.

Erik said nothing but focused on the next checkpoint, which was in the middle of the long bridge to Leader Land.

At the next checkpoint, a slightly younger man in button-down shirt and tie met the group.

"Obviously an Ivy Leaguer," Erik thought. "Looks like a heavy hitter."

As the group stepped back without being told, the second bridge master looked at Erik. "So you want to be a leader, eh?"

"Yes, sir," said Erik, crisply. "I want to be an effective and caring leader."

"That's good to hear," the man said, "but it won't color my evaluation of your answer. I just want you to know that."

"I'm good with that," Erik replied.

"My question to you is this: What's the difference between leadership, management and coaching?"

Again, Erik took his time. "First of all, each is important and should be included as a part of every day. They work in concert with one another, leadership is the influencing, guiding in direction, course, action, opinion. Management means to bring about, to accomplish, to have charge of or responsibility for, to conduct. And finally coaching uses purpose to inspire commitment, stimulate creativity and model accountability.

"Anything else you want to say?" the Ivy League bridge master asked.

"No," Erik said. "I mean, I could go into a more lengthy explanation, but in my estimation and from my own experiences, this is the unique difference."

The man stood for a moment and looked at Erik with the same steely stare of the first bridge master. "Your answer is right on target," he said, swinging open the checkpoint gate.

Again the group cheered as they followed Erik to the last checkpoint on the bridge to Leader Land.

"You're doing great, man," Al said as they walked to the far end of the bridge.

"Thanks," Erik said, looking toward the final checkpoint and his final question before being allowed to enter Leader Land.

At the third checkpoint, a smartly dressed woman appeared as the group approached. "Hello, and welcome," she said, smoothing her pinstriped suit jacket and skirt.

Erik stood at attention as his team stepped back. He was ready for the last question.

The woman was now holding a clipboard and read the question: "What one priority, as a leader, is not negotiable?"

Erik had to think for several seconds before he was ready to deliver his answer. He smoothed the perspiration from his forehead and looked down as he thought. Then he lifted his head and made unmistakable eye contact with the bridge master. "I really think there are three absolute non-negotiables for a leader," he began. "First is to keep my integrity. If my team does not believe me, what difference does what I say make? If I lose my integrity with my team, I will never get anyone to follow me. Second is accepting the responsibilities that come along with leadership – understanding that, no matter what happens or doesn't happen, the leader is responsible for the performance of his team. The third non-negotiable for a leader is that he has to continue to learn while leading. You can't stop learning, even if you reach the highest levels of management."

Every member of his team was smiling.

Erik continued with his answer. "There is a price to be paid to be in Leader Land, yet there are even greater prices to be paid in Management Land. Prices I don't want my team to ever have to pay. At Panic Peak, no one knows where to go or what to do. Confusion rules." At this point, he paused and again wiped the perspiration from his brow. "In the Valley of Comfort, no one ever moves forward because every performance is reduced to mediocrity or worse. The Paperwork Swamp will drown everyone eventually. And in Apathy Cave, no one will ever get anything accomplished. No, I won't be that kind of leader for my team," he concluded.

Al nudged Harry. "Did you hear him say the 'L' word?"

Harry nodded, waiting for the bridge master's response to Erik's answer.

After a moment or two, the bridge master smiled. "Excellent," she said. "You are cleared to visit Leader Land. Just watch your step, as the path is often slippery and uneven. Even the best leaders will sometimes stumble back into Management Land."

By this time, the entire team had surrounded Erik to congratulate him for clearing each of the checkpoints. "Good job, Erik," Angela said.

"Great answers, everyone," Jason assured.

As the group moved past the last checkpoint, Erik looked over his shoulder and was surprised to see a long line of people, snaking across the bridge. "Wow! There are a lot of people trying to cross," he said.

Morgan was the first to speak. "Those who truly want to be an effective leader don't want to spend too much time in Management Land," she explained, "and I think you've learned why. No, everyone who can, everyone who has the right answers and the ability, wants to get to Leader Land. And, as you've noticed, there's only one lane across the bridge – because there's no return traffic. Nobody would knowingly plan to go back to Management Land from Leader Land, but it happens, even to the best leaders. And those making the return trip don't do so voluntarily. For those leaders who slip back, we have a special tunnel that runs under the channel and we send them back to Management Land through a pneumatic tube. It's a quick and painless transport, but those who've had the experience try to avoid that return trip at all costs."

Erik nodded. "I'm glad you explained that to me. I thought the crowds were coming because of some special event."

"In fact, coming to Leader Land is a special event for people who work with other people," Al said. "It's a sort of coming of age, bringing all the knowledge you've gathered throughout your career and learning how to really put it to work."

"Good idea," Erik agreed, but after a few more steps, he stopped abruptly. "I thought you said I would only have to answer three questions," he said to the group.

"Oh, man. This checkpoint is a no-brainer. You'll see," Angela assured.

Just then, an older man stepped out of a guardhouse and met the group at another gate. "Who's the candidate?" he asked, looking over the group and smiling.

Erik stepped forward. "I am," he said.

"Good, good!" the man said, stepping from behind the gate to shake his hand. "So, here's my question. Will you pick up this book and promise to read it?"

"Well, to tell you the truth," Erik stammered. "I'm really not much of a reader. I'm not sure I'll have much extra time for reading now that I've been promoted."

The older man frowned. "I'm sorry to hear that. I'm not sure if anyone told you or not, but crossing the bridge into Leader Land doesn't automatically make it your home from now on. No, no. Indeed not. There are no guarantees just because you cross the bridge. In fact, some of the greatest leaders I can name take return trips to Management Land throughout their careers. You will be next on the return trip itinerary to one of the stops you've just seen in Management Land if you can't make time for reading and more learning. You see, without continued learning, you will unconsciously make decisions that will take you back to Management Land.

"So, since reading and learning isn't on your agenda, I can show you where you can get a ride through the tunnel that goes under the channel … and you can get to Management Land before …."

"Wait. Wait a minute," Erik said, a look of terror crossing his face. "Hey, I know what I said, but I don't want to go back to Management Land. Not now, at least. I mean, I just got here. So I promise I'll make time in my schedule to read a little bit every day. I can read whatever you want me to read, whenever you want me to read it."

"I like your commitment," the older man said, smiling again and handing him the slender brown book he had been holding. "There's no time like the present," the man said, nodding toward the book, "and I know you'll want to set the same example for your team. Learning should never end for you or anyone else who wants to be successful," he added.

Erik eagerly took the book and smiled. "I'll make time," he reassured the man as the checkpoint bridge swung open.

"Welcome to Leader Land," the man said.

As the group moved forward, they passed a sign that read: "Welcome to Leader Land – where we spend our time empowering, sharing, coaching and looking forward to success."

"That's interesting," Erik commented, as they stopped to look at the sign.

"That's what we expect from you," Morgan said, echoing the sign's message. We want to be empowered. We want you to share what you know with us, and show us how to do what you can do. We want to be coached as we seek to accomplish our personal goals, as well as the corporation's mission, and we want you to keep looking forward."

"I can do that," Erik said, remembering times when his own managers kept looking back at their past accomplishments so they could never have a vision for the future.

Morgan smiled and nodded. "That's a relief to hear, but we also want you to know the four requirements we have for you as members of your new team:

1. We want you to hire good people, not just people who look like you or have your same abilities but people who will take our team to the next level.

2. Coach us. We need your guidance and support, and we want to learn how to make even bigger and better contributions to every project. Provide us with a clear vision and a path to success that we can follow.

3. We're going to depend on you to let go people who aren't carrying their weight and are, in reality, holding the rest of the team back from achieving even greater goals.

4. Finally, and this is the biggie: We want you to stay out of
   Management Land. We want a strong visionary and
   conscientious leader."

"Another thing," Al said. "We know communication is important.
And, believe me, every other manager we've had gives
communication a pot full of lip service. But we want more than
communication."

"Yeah, we want connection," Jason continued. "We have great
communication tools – from our computers and handheld
communications devices to Wi-Fi everything. We can all write
great e-mails …."

"Terrific e-mails," Angela said. "But we seemed to have lost the art
of really connecting, and not just with each other. We've lost the
ability to really connect with our customers and the other
departments we work with."

"It's like we've forgotten how to get from the 'me' mentality to the
'we' mentality," Morgan continued. "It's that kind of connection you
need to help us re-learn to use. People follow people, not e-mails,
mission statements, memos. We follow you!"

"Just one more thing," Morgan smiled. "I know we've given you a
pretty long list about what we want – and need – from you, as our
leader, but one of the things this team has been missing for a long
time is the chance to laugh. We think the team that can enjoy
working together, even laughing together, is a measure of the
health of that team, that department and the entire organization,
for that matter."

Erik nodded. "I agree. We spend a lot of our lives at work, so it's important to lighten up, to keep things moving and making it fun, as well."

As they entered Leader Land, the group saw work groups of every variety. There were engineering teams, sales teams, medical groups, publishing houses and accounting firms. There were construction companies, educational groups, high-tech development teams, manufacturing groups and shipping companies, as well as a host of others. And while they all seemed similar to groups Erik had seen before, there was something very different about each one.

"What makes these groups look so different to me?" he finally asked his new team.

"Well, look closely. I mean really closely," said Harry, the senior member of the group. "What do you see?"

"I see people who seem to be happy with what they are doing, some are even celebrating each other."

"Anything else?" Harry wanted to know.

Erik looked around him. "I see people accomplishing, people working very hard but with high energy," came his response. "I also see people going home on time with their work completed."

"But the thing that makes these teams different is that they are connecting. They trust each other and they are more engaged with each other and with their leadership, and vice versa," Harry pointed out.

"So, that's the big difference," Erik said, finally after watching a group for several minutes.

"That's one of the big differences," Harry said, "and that's what we want as a group: to be able to trust each other and to connect – I mean really connect – with you and with each other and our clients.

"The other is they are looking to the future, not living in the past. They may have different responsibilities, may even manage different groups, but they are working toward a common goal, a shared goal. And these people are excited about coming to work because their leader makes them know and feel they make a difference.

"If you look closely," Harry continued, "you'll be able to see that every team member has these five characteristics:

1. Everybody knows what is required of them to excel in their jobs.

2. Everybody knows how they are doing in their individual assignments.

3. Everybody knows their leader is with them, and that their leader cares.

4. Everybody knows how the team is doing and the progress they're making.

5. Everybody knows how and where they fit into the big picture."

"Here's a good example. See Ryan over there?" Jason asked. "He just arrived on the job and his team has increased productivity by 30 percent. Know why?"

Erik shrugged his shoulders. "Because Ryan is a super-producer?"

"Well, that, too," said Jason, "but mainly because the leader is proactive. His team saw Ryan's arrival as an opportunity for the entire group to try a totally new approach to a battle they've waged for several months. By adding Ryan's tools to those already in place, not only did they resolve the problem and clear the hurdle, they began seeing more results for the same amount of effort. In other words, a win-win-win situation. Ryan won, the team won and the customers won."

"Awesome!" Erik replied. "That's why I want to hit the ground running with you guys. I see so much talent, so much potential, and I think you've barely scratched the surface."

"Finally," Angela exclaimed. "I've been waiting two years to hear someone say that, but I want to add one more thing. You know me, there's always one more thing."

The group laughed. "That's our Angie."

"So, what did you want to add?" Erik said, turning to his new employee.

"We want you to be the authority," she said. "We need to know who's in charge … and that's your job. Don't make us second guess that."

"Okay. That's another promise I'll make here and now. I'll be the authority, which also means the buck stops with me. And while I'll always be happy to receive the kudos, I'll also take the criticism for our group."

Angela smiled. "That's a relief. We've wasted a lot of time in the past, wondering if our manager really had the authority we needed and whether we should follow his direction or wait until something was handed down from higher up. It made my job confusing, and I think I can speak for the entire team on that one."

The group nodded in agreement.

As Erik and his team walked on, they saw another group … except one of the team members was sitting off to the side by herself.

"What's the story here?" Erik wanted to know.

"You tell us," Harry said.

"Well, a good leader is going to be proactive when it comes to developing new strategies and new projects," Erik began. "But, if I remember correctly from one of my mentors, a good leader not only has to take the time to plan a strategy with the team, he or she also has to stop periodically and reflect on what's working and to understand what's not working and take that out of the picture."

"Right you are," said a voice coming from the office sitting just ahead. "Proactive reflection is the key to continuous improvement. If something's not working, quit using that approach; and if something is working well, keep doing it and expand on it whenever or wherever possible. Oh, by the way, my name's Jack, and I'm one of the Leader Land regulars. There aren't too many of us because it's pretty hard to stay here on an ongoing basis. Most leaders have lapses of one kind or another, but those of us who are regulars try to keep things on the smooth here. Even if I do say so myself, we're doing a pretty good job."

"Lapses?"

"No leader is immune to sliding backward, even the best of us. Here's a good example," Jack began. "One group – terrifically talented, as I recall – began coming up with great ideas that would not only increase production but streamline the process leading up to it.

Their leader, who had worked his way up, remembered seeing upper management's disdain for change. He finally diluted their plan down to where nothing really changed and production remained a flat line, so he ended up in the Valley of Comfort over in Management Land. Be forewarned – even the best can backslide from time to time.

"Another talented leader – and it's been awhile, so I've forgotten his name – lost his team because he didn't think everything he did would count. As the leader, everything counts!

"On one occasion, he met with a team member and confided, 'Those people upstairs don't have a clue about what we're doing. They're leading us in the wrong direction, but don't tell the others on the team I think this whole campaign stinks.'

"That manager didn't think his confiding in one team member amounted to anything, but, hey, he was the leader and with his team looking to him for direction, everything he did counted, including his lack of respect for corporate decision makers. Think about it. That guy put that one team member – and once the story got out, the rest of his team – in a really bad position. Like, who were they supposed to believe?"

"Oh, man," Erik said. "I see your point," he added, trying to absorb every word Jack shared.

"Another leader, seeing the success of his existing team, tried to discourage anyone from leaving, although several in the group had the ability to move ahead."

"Been there," Harry reminded.

"And, in another group, the manager was so conscientious about communicating, that many of his team spent more time answering and distributing e-mails than really focusing on first things first," Jack continued. "Instead of using technology to the team's advantage, it actually created another hurdle."

"We call those overly zealous e-mailers 'weapons of mass distraction,'" Morgan offered.

"Here's another thing," Jack said, captivating the entire group with his energy. "I've thought about this many times in my tenure, but wouldn't it be great if everyone on the team was always as productive as they are on the day before they go on vacation?"

Erik and his team were silent, but only for a moment.

"I know I'm more focused, more efficient and more organized the day before I leave on vacation because I know how much I need to accomplish before I leave," Morgan nodded, "and I have just so much time to complete my to-do list."

"Exactly!" Jack smiled. "But, just imagine if every one of you had that concentration, that focus, that energy and were that organized, not just the day before vacation but every other day of the year. Imagine where you could be and how much closer you could be to reaching your ultimate goals."

"Man, that's something to think about," Harry said. "I've never thought of it in those terms before, but that's really a great concept."

"It's something we all need to talk about," Erik agreed. "I've seen it 100 times but never thought to translate it to the every day. Great idea," he said, beaming at his new mentor.

"One more war story and then I have to run," Jack promised. "One leader did a great job with his team, paving the way as they all achieved success, except for the leader's one Achilles heel. He never quite got around to giving regular performance reviews on time, which he felt was a small detail because he did such a great job of rewarding his team and communicating his appreciation for their work.

"Except, of course, their pay increases were probably pretty closely tied to those performance reviews, which sent mixed and confusing messages to his team, even though he was letting them know how important they were.

"Exactly," Jack said, extending his hand to Erik. "Welcome to Leader Land. Hope to see you again. This is a great place."

"I'll say," Erik said. "I'm really impressed."

"Well, don't spend too much time being too impressed because as a leader, you always need to spend your time where it brings the best results, and that time is with your team, as a group and individually," Jack said. "Well, I still have lots to do. I'll say goodbye for now, but drop by anytime. Oh, I almost forgot. One more thing: Learn from past experiences and past performances. Notice I said *learn* from them, not *dwell* on them. As leaders, we always want our focus to be on the future and what we can do to improve where we are."

"Thanks for sharing that. Those are both well worth remembering and using with my team. I will come back just as soon as I can, so thanks for the invitation," Erik said.

"Jack's been here for a long time. He's a great guy," Harry said. "One of the best."

"Proactive reflection," Erik repeated. "That's the key. I'm going to remember that."

As they continued walking, Morgan was the next to speak. "Well, Erik, we're close to the end of our journey. But we need your assurance on several points."

"Okay, shoot."

"Are you willing to spend time not just communicating but connecting with us?" she asked.

"I will definitely make that another top priority," he promised.

"And are you committed to giving follow-up and coaching on the personal development plans on a consistent and regular basis?" Jason wondered.

"Absolutely. I know how important these reviews are to both of us, but let's focus our time on your proactive coaching and planning so we can get you to the next level," said Erik.

"What about office protocols?" Angela questioned. "Are you going to get out of your cushy office and find out about what's going on in the real world?"

"Done," Erik said.

"And will you be willing to let people go if they're not moving our team forward?" asked Al.

"I'll let employees go when I see personal goals are in conflict with team goals, or for other reasons if they come up," Erik said. "And

I'll also do my best to get out of your way with unnecessary reports and paperwork that keeps you from doing what you do best."

"One more thing," said Harry, his tone and expression serious. "Will you have the courage to tell upper management what needs to happen so we can continue moving forward?"

"Absolutely. I'm not as afraid of change as I am of status quo burning us all out."

"Welcome to our team," Jason said, extending his hand as the rest of the team crowded around. "It's been good traveling with you this far."

"I hope we'll be able to travel many more roads together, as long as we're not visiting Management Land," Erik laughed. "But, hey, I do have one more question."

Jason's face was serious. "Okay. What's up?"

"Yesterday there was a note on my desk. No signature. No markings of any kind, and it said something about, 'Are you like all the others?' Maybe you all can help me solve the mystery."

The group was quiet for a moment. Then Morgan stepped forward. "I think you could say it was our invitation for this journey today," she said, looking guilty but still focused on their mission. "We want it to be the beginning of great opportunities for all of us."

Now Erik understood. "I think we share that goal. But if you have any doubts at any time, let's talk. I do think you could say this new team is off to an amazing start."

Leader Land

Observations

♦ People are more proactive and seek new challenges.

♦ Team members maintain clear focus and direction.

♦ Everyone listens and connects while communicating.

♦ Leaders recognize and reward accomplishments.

♦ Leaders understand that it's difficult to stay in Leader Land and continually evaluate how to stay out of Management Land.

Actions

♦ Identify where you are today by self-assessment, by having your team assess you, and by asking your boss to assess you. Then, turn that feedback into change.

♦ Commit to your personal development by creating your individual coaching plan. Start with your behavioral strengths and developmental areas, your skill-set strengths and developmental needs, personal and professional goals and identifying what is "the main thing." Then, develop actions and milestones in a committed, developmental timetable.

Results

♦ Your team will be focused, energized and committed.

♦ Every effort will be a learning opportunity and results-oriented.

♦ Team members will eagerly take ownership of strategies.

♦ Every team member will have an opportunity for feedback and the ability to grow.

♦ Everyone wins!

BACK TO REALITY

Early the next morning, Erik awakened from what he thought had been a fitful night's sleep. But, strangely, he was feeling not only refreshed, but also energized.

As he bound out of bed, he stopped to kiss his wife and hugged her for several moments. "I'm going to be the best manager, I mean leader, this team has ever seen," he said. "I'm ready to get to know them and start planning our next steps together. I have a great team."

"How do you know that?" she asked quizzically.

"Uh, well, I just know," he said. "Somehow, I just know it."

After breakfast, he couldn't wait to get to the office and get started. "I'll begin with a team meeting," Erik decided as he drove to work. "I need to sit down with them, as a group and separately, to hear about what they're doing and what their priorities are. I need to connect."

As he was unpacking a few things in his office, Sherry Bryant, manager of the accounting group, poked her head in the door. "Welcome aboard," she said. "Glad to have you."

"Thanks," Erik said, setting down the last stack of books from the packing boxes. "I'm looking forward to the challenge, but I do have a lot to learn. One of the areas I haven't read anything about is the team's performance reviews. How are those usually done up here?"

"Well, the short answer is whenever you get around to it," said the senior manager. "If I overlook one, I usually hear from the team member after a while. That's when it becomes a priority."

"Oh, just wondered," said Erik as he sat down at his first for the first time. "There's no regular schedule?"

"I guess that would be up to the manager. I just hate to reward one member of the team if I can't reward everyone," she explained. "Well, I need to get to a meeting but wanted to stop by and say 'Welcome!'"

"Thanks, Sherry. Hey, ever heard of a place called 'Management Land?'"

"Is that a new TV show?"

"I'm not sure," he smiled. "Just wondered if you'd ever heard of it."

"Don't think so. Let's have lunch … soon," she said as she closed the door behind her.

As the team met for the first time, Erik felt a strange but close kinship to each member of the group. "It's like we've known each other before," he said to himself as shook hands with Al, Angela, Morgan, Jason and Harry.

During the meeting, Erik decided he would set the pace with some commitments he thought were very important. The sheets he handed to his team bore his signature and the following list:

As team leader I commit to the following:

♦ To develop each team member to his or her full potential.

♦ To seek new challenges for all of us.

♦ To provide each of you with a clear focus and direction.

♦ To connect and communicate.

♦ To provide appropriate recognition of individual and group accomplishment

♦ To make learning the highest priority for all of us.

♦ To learn from the past and focus on the future.

♦ To work to become proactive in every aspect of our work.

After the meeting, he began jotting down their projects and some team priorities. "Yes," he said to himself. "This is going to be the best team in the company. Just give me a few weeks to earn your trust, listen to your input and jointly develop our plan."

Just then, Max Johnson, a fellow manager stopped by. "Hey, guy. What's up?" he asked. "Ready for the company golf tournament?"

"I'm afraid my golf game isn't really as good as I want it to be before I have to embarrass myself in front of the entire company," Erik apologized, "and I'm trying to keep first things first, seeing is how this is my first team to lead."

"Awe, management's simple," Johnson reassured. "You'll always have your stars and, well, the others."

"Maybe," Erik said, "or I may just have a whole team of stars. Who knows?"

"Yeah," Johnson said, not quite sure how to respond. "Who knows? Well, see you 'round."

"Hey," Erik said as Johnson was leaving, "Ever heard of Management Land?"

"Nope," Johnson said, "but I don't read much. Don't have time. Feel like I'm on a treadmill."

"Just wondered," replied Erik, getting back to his work. And then he stopped, put down his pencil and leaned back, his hands behind his head. "I thought it was a dream," he said to himself. "Yeah, it had to be a dream. Management Land. Leader Land. Must have been my imagination working overtime."

Then one of the most influential people in the company, vice president Jeff Walters, came into his office.

"Welcome to the leadership team," he beamed. "We have watched you prepare for this opportunity for years. You've earned this promotion. I am proud to have you on our team. Please accept this book as my congratulatory gift. I hope you will take the time to read it. It may come in handy somewhere along the way."

"Before you leave, could you tell me what you think is the key to your success?" Erik asked.

"Erik, I think the book I just gave you will answer that question. Why don't you read it and then we can discuss what you discover?"

After he left, I opened the book that he gave me – *Monday Morning Mentoring* – and noticed that he had written a personal note to me:

> *Dear Erik,*
>
> *Congratulations on your new promotion into leadership.*
>
> *You are about to enter a wonderful period of your life. Now the learning really begins.*
>
> *If you ever want to talk about personal or business issues, I would be honored to allow you to learn from my experiences. You just have to ask.*
>
> *Best wishes,*
> *Jeff Walters*

As I flipped through the book, I noticed it was written to Jeff Walters from his mentor. Then I smiled as I saw the title of the third chapter: *Escape From Management Land.*

Maybe it wasn't my imagination …

A FINAL WORD

Escape From Management Land is a fantasy filled with real-life situations. While most leaders will not actually visit a place called Management Land, they, inevitably, will fall into the traps described in this tale.

Every year, leadership deficiencies cost companies billions of dollars. The expenses associated with turnover, morale issues, decreased productivity, sexual harassment charges, abusive behavior, and ineffective communication are all leadership failures that carry very expensive price tags.

Your team deserves more.

They deserve to work in an environment that allows them to be successful. They deserve to have their problems solved and to understand what changes they can make to improve. They deserve to be treated with respect and to receive credit for their success. They deserve to be led by individuals who are positive role models.

Leadership is not something to be taken lightly. It is an important and valuable commodity for any organization. Leadership is not something that you can buy. It can't be inherited. It cannot be given to you as a gift. It cannot be stolen from someone else who has it. And it cannot be inherited with a promotion.

There is no easy path to leadership. It has to be earned!

- ♦ By accepting responsibility to become the very best
- ♦ By surrounding yourself with committed people
- ♦ By creating a guiding vision for others to follow
- ♦ By communicating with crystal clear clarity
- ♦ By overcoming adversity that comes our way
- ♦ By being optimistic and looking for the best in others
- ♦ By empowering others to do what they do best
- ♦ By making positive changes
- ♦ By having the courage to do what's right
- ♦ By leading by your example
- ♦ By preparing yourself and your people for the future

Leadership success cannot be measured solely by the corporate bottom line. Although profitability is important and necessary, your ultimate success is in the legacy you leave for others to follow. Our sincere desire is that the lessons described in this book will impact your leadership legacy.

Your goal should be to seize every moment and passionately pursue life by being the very best you can be. No looking back. No regrets!

Whatever you do, wherever you are and wherever you go, you are a leader with influence far greater than you will probably ever be able to comprehend. Your leadership shadow is constant, influencing others even when you are not aware that anyone is watching. *You do make a difference!*

Best wishes, as you become the leader you want to be!

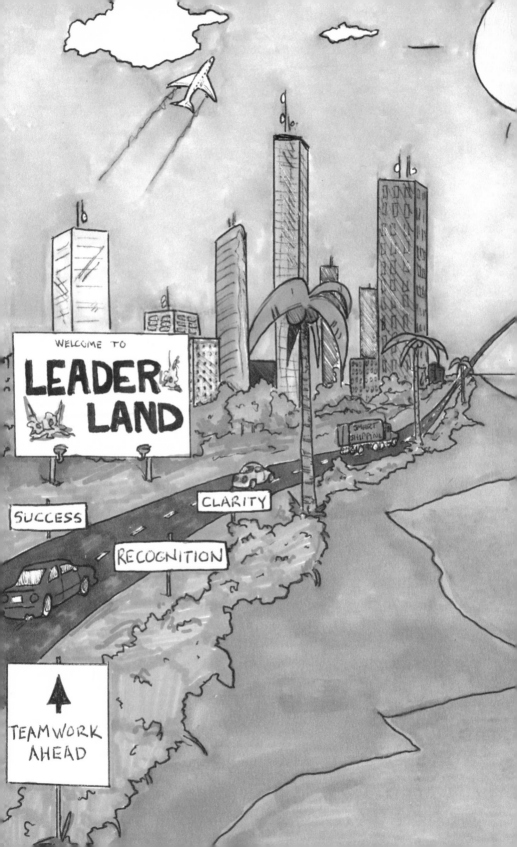

ACCELERATE POWERFUL
LEADERSHIP PACKAGE $199⁹⁵

Monday Morning Mentoring is an expanded and enhanced hardcover version of best-selling *Monday Morning Leadership*. It includes new sessions on how to deal with change and constructive feedback. **$19.95**

Monday Morning Leadership is David Cottrell's best-selling book. It offers unique encouragement and direction that will help you become a better manager, employee, and person. **$14.95**

7 Moments … That Define Excellent Leaders: The difference between average and excellent can be found in moments … literally. These moments shape the leaders we are and the leaders we will become. Seize the moment to read and apply, and you will be one step closer to leadership excellence! **$14.95**

Sticking to It: The Art of Adherence offers practical steps to help you consistently execute your plans. Read it and WIN! **$9.95**

Escape from Management Land teaches important lessons about leadership that will help you decide if you're willing to do what it takes to escape Management Land and move into Leader Land. **$14.95**

The Leadership Secrets of Santa Claus helps your team accomplish "big things" by giving employees clear goals, solid accountabilities, feedback, coaching, and recognition in your "workshop." **$14.95**

Management Insights explores the myths and realities of management. It provides insight into how you can become a successful manager. **$14.95**

Listen Up, Leader! Ever wonder what employees think about their leaders? This book tells you the seven characteristics of leadership that people will follow. **$9.95**

Monday Morning Leadership for Women is an inspirational story about a manager and her mentor. It provides insights and wisdom for dealing with leadership issues that are unique to women. **$14.95**

Leadership ER is a powerful story that shares valuable insights on how to achieve and maintain personal health, business health and the critical balance between the two. **$14.95**

Leadership ... Biblically Speaking connects practical applications with scriptural guidance on how to address today's business and personal issues. **$19.95**

Leadership Courage identifies 11 acts of courage required for effective leadership and provides practical steps on how to become a courageous leader. **$14.95**

Birdies, Pars & Bogeys: Leadership Lessons from the Links is an excellent gift for the golfing executive. Zig Ziglar praises it as "concise, precise, insightful, inspirational, informative." **$14.95**

The Best Leadership Advice I Ever Got is a compilation of 75 CEOs, presidents, professors, politicians, and others leaders describing the best advice they received that helped them become effective leaders! **$14.95**

The NEW CornerStone Perpetual Calendar, a compelling collection of quotes about leadership and life, is perfect for office desks, school and home countertops. **$14.95**

The CornerStone Leadership Collection of Cards is designed to make it easy for you to show appreciation for your team, clients and friends. The awesome photography and your personal message written inside will create a lasting impact. Pack of 12 (12 styles/1 each) **$24.95**
Posters also available.

Monday Morning Leadership 360° Online Profile To order, visit www.CornerStoneLeadership.com **$99.95**

Visit www.**CornerStoneLeadership**.com for additional books and resources.

☑ **YES! Please send me extra copies of *Escape from Management Land!***
1-30 copies $14.95   31-100 copies $13.95   101+ copies $12.95

Escape from Management Land _____ copies X _____ = $ _____

Escape from Management Land PowerPoint™ _____ copies X $99.95 = $ _____

Additional Leadership Development Resources

Accelerate Powerful Leadership Package _____ pack(s) X $199.95 = $ _____
(Includes all items on page 117-118.)

Other Books

_____ _____ copies X _____ = $ _____

_____ _____ copies X _____ = $ _____

_____ _____ copies X _____ = $ _____

Shipping & Handling $ _____

Subtotal $ _____

Sales Tax (8.25%-TX Only) $ _____

Total (U.S. Dollars Only) $ _____

Shipping and Handling Charges

Total $ Amount	Up to $49	$50-$99	$100-$249	$250-$1199	$1200-$2999	$3000+
Charge	$6	$9	$16	$30	$80	$125

Name _____ Job Title _____

Organization _____ Phone _____

Shipping Address _____ Fax _____

Billing Address _____ E-mail _____
(required when ordering PowerPoint® Presentation)

City _____ State _____ ZIP _____

❏ Please invoice (Orders over $200) Purchase Order Number (if applicable) _____

Charge Your Order: ❏ MasterCard ❏ Visa ❏ American Express

Credit Card Number _____ Exp. Date _____

Signature _____

❏ Check Enclosed (Payable to: CornerStone Leadership)

Fax	**Mail**	**Phone**
972.274.2884	P.O. Box 764087	888.789.5323
	Dallas, TX 75376	

www.**CornerStoneLeadership**.com

Thank you for reading *Escape from Management Land.*
We hope it has assisted you in your quest for
personal and professional growth.

CornerStone Leadership is committed to provide new
and enlightening products to organizations worldwide.
Our mission is to fuel knowledge with practical resources
that will accelerate your team's productivity,
success and job satisfaction!

Best wishes for your continued success.

CornerStone
Leadership Institute
www.CornerStoneLeadership.com

*Start a crusade in your organization –
have the courage to learn, the vision to lead,
and the passion to share.*